# Hope For Haiti

## An Account of Pastor Jean Jacob Paul And Reformation Hope, Inc.

By

Martin L. Hawley, MAET, MDiv
Executive Director, Reformation Hope, Inc.

Wild Olive Press, Woodstock, Georgia
November 2013

# Table of Contents

Dedication and Appreciation . . . . . . . . . . . . . . . . . . . . . . . . . . . . . . . . iv

Note to the Reader. . . . . . . . . . . . . . . . . . . . . . . . . . . . . . . . . . . . . . . . vi

*Mwen se Ayiti* . . . . . . . . . . . . . . . . . . . . . . . . . . . . . . . . . . . . . . . . . . vii

Introduction . . . . . . . . . . . . . . . . . . . . . . . . . . . . . . . . . . . . . . . . . . . . ix

I.   Mission Context: God Prepares Haiti for the Gospel . . . . . . . . . . 1

II.  Mission Calling: God Returns an American Citizen to Haiti . . . 25

III. Mission Focus: Caring for the Orphaned Children of Haiti . . . . .35

IV.  Mission Organization: God Calls Reformation Hope
     Into Being . . . . . . . . . . . . . . . . . . . . . . . . . . . . . . . . . . . . . . . . . . 49

V.   Mission Disaster: Earthquake! January 12, 2010 . . . . . . . . . . . 55

VI.  Mission Preaching — You Aren't In Kansas Anymore! . . . . . . . 65

VII. Mission Challenge: Voodoo and Catholicism In Haiti . . . . . . . 75

VIII. Mission Reprise: Rebuilding Hope In Haiti . . . . . . . . . . . . . . . 91

IX.  Mission Shifts: Establishing Sustainable Mission Methods . . . 101

X.   Mission Teamwork: Forging Strategic Partnerships . . . . . . . . 107

XI.  Mission Issues: Short-Term Challenges —
     Long-Term Solutions. . . . . . . . . . . . . . . . . . . . . . . . . . . . . . . . . 117

XII. Mission Transformed: An Indigenous Way Ahead . . . . . . . . . 129

XIII. Epilogue: Mission Customs and Mission Crises . . . . . . . . . . . 133

Bibliography. . . . . . . . . . . . . . . . . . . . . . . . . . . . . . . . . . . . . . . . . . . . 147

καὶ ᾄδουσιν ᾠδὴν καινὴν λέγοντες· Ἄξιος εἶ λαβεῖν τὸ βιβλίον
καὶ ἀνοῖξαι τὰς σφραγῖδας αὐτοῦ, ὅτι ἐσφάγης καὶ ἠγόρασας
τῷ θεῷ ἐν τῷ αἵματί σου ἐκ πάσης φυλῆς καὶ γλώσσης καὶ λαοῦ
καὶ ἔθνους, καὶ ἐποίησας αὐτοὺς τῷ θεῷ ἡμῶν βασιλείαν καὶ
ἱερεῖς, καὶ βασιλεύουσιν ἐπὶ τῆς γῆς.

*And they sang a new song, saying,*
*"Worthy are you to take the scroll and to open its seals, for*
*you were slain, and by your blood you ransomed people for*
*God from every tribe and language and people and nation,*
*and you have made them a kingdom and priests to our God,*
*and they shall reign on the earth."*
*(Revelation 5:9—10)*

# Dedication and Appreciation

This work is dedicated to the glory of God, who has made us all in his image, to our Lord Jesus Christ, who is the Redeemer and King of the nations, and to the Holy Spirit, who continues building a kingdom and priests upon the earth from every tribe, language, people-group and nation around the globe. Truly the gates of hell itself shall not prevail against it.

The author expresses the deepest appreciation to Pastor Jean Jacob Paul, God's unique instrument in Haiti, and a true brother in Christ. Thanks is also due to the dedicated team of Haitians who serve the Souls Winning Ministry Orphanage in La Plaine, Haiti, and to the many volunteers and committed board members of Reformation Hope, Inc., based in Marietta, Georgia. I am also deeply thankful for my wife, Shari, who assisted with the editing of the manuscript, designed the cover, created the formatting, and generally put up with me throughout the process.

# Note to the Reader

## Creole Variant Spellings

The reader will notice that some words appear in this text with variations in spelling from the author's usage to various usages (or lexicography) from sources cited. For many years the world lacked a standardized spelling form for Haitian Creole (Kreyol), with a number of systems in use. Also, in Haiti there are variations in Creole usage from one region to another. Thus, in this work multiple spelling forms will be found for the names of Voodoo gods or spirits, for Voodoo itself, and for some Creole expressions.

The two terms that will be encountered most often with variations are lwa, the word for a Voodoo spirit or god, which is also rendered as loa or l'wha, and Voodoo (the African-derived religion of Haiti), which is also spelled by writers and scholars as *Vodou, Vodun, Vodoun, Vaudou,* and *Vaudoux*.

## Abbreviations

Throughout this work, various forms for the name of the Reformation Hope, Incorporated 501(c)(3) organization are employed. Thus Reformation Hope also appears as Ref Hope and RHI.

## Locations

The Souls Winning Ministries Orphanage is located in a suburb of Haiti named Marin, which is also part of a larger region known as La Plaine. Both of these terms for the main mission compound are employed in this work.

# *Mwen se Ayiti*
by Dave Wright

The earth opens to never speak in vain but speaks
Sons and Daughters, speak Ayiti —
Speak Land of High Mountains

Ayiti? you...
Le Cathedrale de Port-au-Prince, the footings?
The cupola of the north tower, beacon
Light for the Haitian Mariner?
Le Palais National once facing Place L'Ouverture?

Ayiti speak if not these fallen places?

The Caribbean gate in Greater Antilles?
The first door of a new world?
The cruise port of a luxury liner?

Speak Ayiti, speak to fat fish in your harbors!

Not in vain but speak Sons and Daughters,
Moun Lan!
The earth opens speak walls away, reveals
Mountains reveal you, the homeland
Never forsakes the home, the people
Never Moun Lan! Never home.

Ayiti, kouman ou ye?[1]

...

"Mwen se Ayiti
Mwen se Ayiti:
Land of High Mountains

I am Home."[2]

---

1  Creole for, "Haiti, how are you?"
2  Dave Wright, "Mwen se Ayiti." In *Vwa: Poems for Haiti*, Lisa Marie Basile, ed. (Caper Literary Journal Charity Project, CreateSpace Independent Publishing Platform, March 16, 2010), 33 – 34.

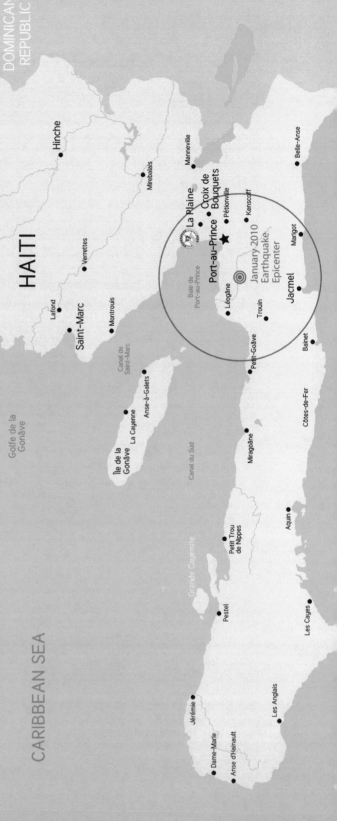

ATLANTIC OCEAN

DOMINICAN REPUBLIC

HAITI

The Nation of Haiti occupies the western third of the island of Hispaniola. It is a country whose landscape is largely shaped by rugged mountains and coastal features. Several important rivers also add character, especially in the central and northern regions. The capitol of Haiti is Port-au-Prince.

CARIBBEAN SEA

Île de la Tortue

Môle Saint-Nicolas

Baie de Henne

Port-de-Paix

Le Borgne

Cap-Haïtien

Limbé

Ennery

Gonaïves

Grande-Rivière-du-Nord

Saint-Raphaël

Fort Liberté

Hinche

Mirebalais

Manneville

Belle-Anse

Lafond

Verrettes

Saint-Marc

Montrouis

La Plaine

Croix de Bouquets

Pétionville

Kenscoff

Port-au-Prince

January 2010 Earthquake Epicenter

Margot

Léogâne

Trouin

Jacmel

Bainet

Baie de Port-au-Prince

Golfe de la Gonâve

Canal de Saint-Marc

Anse-à-Galets

La Cayenne

Île de la Gonâve

Canal du Sud

Petit-Goâve

Côtes-de-Fer

Miragoâne

Grande Cayemite

Petit Trou de Nippes

Aquin

Pestel

Les Cayes

Jérémie

Dame-Marie

Anse d'Hainault

Les Anglais

# Introduction

The purpose for this work, *Mission and Development in Haiti: An Account of Pastor Jean Jacob Paul and Reformation Hope, Inc.*, is to provide an accurate account of God's working through Haitian-American pastor Jean Jacob Paul, Souls Winning Ministries, and Reformation Despoir D'Haiti, partnering with Reformation Hope, Incorporated (RHI), a U.S.-based mission and development organization. Yet for such an account to be of interest or of use to those unconnected with Reformed kingdom mission among the people of Haiti, this account must lead to analysis, and the analysis to practical application.

Anyone who has ventured to answer God's call and travel to a Third World environment like that of Haiti — whether short-term or long-term — recognizes that a host of challenges awaits them. Likewise, those who sense that the Lord is leading them to establish a sending agency in the United States to serve a mission field such as Haiti or the Dominican Republic may also understand that a long road lies ahead, fraught with many hurdles and learning curves.

After more than seven years of partnering with the people of Haiti, Reformation Hope has made its share of mistakes along that long road. While there are many, many obvious signs of God's favor, yet there are also some scars from hard-won lessons — wisdom gained — which must be shared in the sincere hope that others called to serve with Haitians or other people groups may avoid some of those same mistakes.

With this very practical purpose in mind, the following chapters of this work are organized topically and include an introductory illustration, further accounts and pertinent facts, appropriate analysis, and then conclusions as to how to apply the lessons learned within the topic to future kingdom mission partnerships. The illustrations used with reference to each topic are derived from the experiences of pastor Jean Jacob Paul, as well as from the author of this work and others who have served with Reformation Hope. In order to provide the reader with a broader perspective on the richly nuanced Haitian mission field, this work also relies upon resources and references provided by others who have served or are presently serving, as well as views of the Haitians themselves.

*Haiti's Presidential Palace in Port-au-Prince, until the 2010 earthquake, was the most recognizable structure in the nation's capitol.*

*For my days pass away like smoke,*
*and my bones burn like a furnace.*
*My heart is struck down like grass and has withered;*
*I forget to eat my bread.*
*Because of my loud groaning my bones cling to my flesh.*
*I am like a desert owl of the wilderness,*
*like an owl of the waste places;*
*I lie awake; I am like a lonely sparrow*
*on the housetop. All the day my enemies taunt me; those who*
*deride me use my name for a curse.*
*For I eat ashes like bread and mingle tears with my drink,*
*because of your indignation and anger; for you have taken*
*me up and thrown me down. My days are like an evening*
*shadow; I wither away like grass.*
*But you, O Lord, are enthroned forever;*
*you are remembered throughout all generations.*
*You will arise and have pity on Zion; it is the time to favor*
*her; the appointed time has come. For your servants hold her*
*stones dear and have pity on her dust.*
*(Psalm 102:3 – 14)*

# CHAPTER I
# Mission Context: God Prepares Haiti For the Gospel

The Haitian Revolution is an event of global significance partly because of where it took place. Eighteenth-century Saint-Domingue represented the apogee of the European colonizing process begun three centuries earlier. In the late 1780s, it was the world's major exporter of sugar, coffee, and, till shortly before, of indigo as well. These were not the cheap bulk commodities they later became but were valuable staples, the lifeblood of Atlantic commerce. Saint-Domingue's exports were worth far more than the gold of Brazil or the silver of Mexico, and they kept an entire navy in business. The colony's enslaved population was then almost as large as that of the United States south of the Potomac.

It had become the single main destination of the Atlantic slave trade. When the French Revolution broke out, Saint-Domingue was home to almost half a million slaves, about 30,000 white colonists, and a roughly equal number of free people of color.[3]

It is an all too common occurrence for Christians to enter a short-term or even a long-term mission field, without grappling with the historical texture which has shaped the culture they seek to serve. Whether the target field is Haiti, Yemen, or Tibetan China, a serious effort must be made to open the annals of history for that particular people group.

Why is this so important? Well, in the first place, people guided by the Bible understand that God has been at work in every place of intended mission, preparing people through the events of prior centuries, decades, and years. Without an understanding of the historical background of a particular culture, the missional servant lacks key pieces of information necessary for bringing the Gospel to bear in redeeming those areas of the culture most in need. Without at least a cursory familiarity with historical milieu, the missionary is in danger of misreading current events as they unfold before their very eyes — not to mention misreading the very people God has called them to serve. Accurately assessing and then contextually evangelizing the culture is impossible without a grasp of its history.

The nation now known as Haiti is a foremost example illustrating the importance of studying God's working through history in order to prepare a people and a place to receive the Gospel. Those who board a modern jet aircraft bound for Haiti from the prosperous nations of Canada, France, and the United States without paying heed to its history are beginning their kingdom service at a great disadvantage. Arriving in Port-au-Prince and mingling with a proud people shaped by a rich heritage, while ignorant of the historical context may well do far more harm than good.

Much of what goes on in Haiti today, from the repeating patterns of violence, the instability and despotism in governments, the depletion of resources, the poverty of most of its people, and the co-dependent

---

3 David Patrick Geggus, "Saint-Domingue on the Eve of the Haitian Revolution," in *Haitian History: New Perspectives*, Alyssa Goldstein Sepinwall, ed. (New York, NY: Routledge Press, 2013), 72.

relationships between it and nations of the developed world can be identified as the outworking of its long, tumultuous history.

Originally part of the large Spanish colonial possession of Hispaniola (later Santo Domingo), Haiti was discovered by the European powers with the arrival of the explorer Christopher Columbus in 1492. After Columbus' original settlement of Navidad, located near present-day Cap-Haïtien, was destroyed by the native population, the explorer established another outpost, Isabela, in 1493 during his second expedition.

Contact with the ever-increasing numbers of Spanish colonizers quickly brought about the exterminations of the indigenous Taíno people, who were vulnerable to the European diseases previously unknown in the Western Hemisphere. In order to continue developing the resources available to them from this rich island, the Spanish authorities began the importation of large numbers of slaves from the western and central regions of Africa, including Angola, the Bight of Benin and the Congo.

Through the Treaty of Ryswick in 1697 an increasing French hegemony over the western third of Santo Domingo was recognized by Spain and the exploitation of what became known as Saint Domingue's resources through a plantation and basic industrial economy grew substantially — as did the population of African slaves necessary for processing the profitable sugar, coffee, and indigo for export.

According to some scholars of Haitian history, it was the increasing number of colonial plantations and the peculiarities of French slave law which began the process of extensive deforestation in Haiti and other problems that continue today. John Garrigus writes:

> The conditions of Saint-Domingue's proto-industrial plantation system also explain another of Haiti's modern environmental problems: micro-farming. Many Haitian peasant farmers support their families on less than two acres (0.75 hectares) of land. ... the Code Noir of 1685, obligated owners to provide their slaves with a specified minimum amount of food. By the mid-1700s, however, Saint-Domingue's planters had discovered that it was cheaper to give slaves garden plots and let them grow most of their own provisions. These plots became vital to the survival of enslaved workers, allowing some to escape malnutrition and even to enter the local economy. Slave gardeners produced much of the food

available in colonial markets. Gardens became synonymous with autonomy, even freedom. After the great slave revolt of August 1791, as rebel leaders tried to negotiate with colonial authorities, their primary demand was not emancipation, but three days a week to work their gardens. The end of slavery in 1794, Haitian independence in 1804, and the end of the threat of a French invasion in 1825 produces an exodus from the plantations.[4]

The consequences of clearing large tracks of land in the plains of Haiti for sugar cane and indigo cultivation, the increasing number of coffee plantations removing the native trees from the mountainsides, and the subdivision of other land among the hundreds of thousands of slaves for micro-farming, can be seen today in the barren, erosion-prone slopes and in the difficulty Haitians face in feeding their large population. (Deforestation in Haiti continued into the early 2000s as its people cut down remaining trees for housing and especially for cooking fuel.)[5]

The revolution which took place in Saint-Domingue (Haiti) was the first successful slave revolt in the western hemisphere. Its roots were quite complicated and had as much to do with the population of prosperous free persons of color and a number of progressive whites, as it did the many thousands of slaves on the great plantations. Both the American and French Revolutions no doubt impacted the thinking and the timing of the island revolution which would lead to the creation of the nation of Haiti. In fact, some of the later leaders of the successful insurrection

---

4 *French colonists observed dramatic environmental changes caused by deforestation and understood that the expansion of plantation agriculture was to blame.* John D. Garrigus, "The Legacies of Pre-revolutionary Saint-Domingue," in *Haiti Rising: Haitian History, Culture and the Earthquake of 2010*, Martin Munro, ed. (Kingston, Jamaica: University of the West Indies Press, 2010), 117 – 118. See his article for more details on the process of plantation deforestation through the 17th and 18th centuries in Haiti.

5 *As recently as fifty years ago, Haiti's forests were thriving and trees covered 60 percent of the country. Today, less than one percent of Haiti remains forested.* The Lambi Fund, is seeking to guide and fund reforestation in Haiti. http://www.lambifund.org/programs_reforestation.shtml. Pastor Jean Paul often recalls that when he was small boy in Haiti in the mid-1960s, the country still had large forested areas in many places.

were personally involved in helping the American colonies gain their independence.

The War of Independence had perhaps its greatest impact on the free community of African descent. A special regiment of free coloreds was raised and sent to Georgia to fight alongside the rebel colonists. It included André Rigaud, Jean-Baptiste Chavannes, J.-B. Villatte, Henry Christophe, Jean-Pierre Lambert, and Louis-Jacques Bauvais; its muster roll read like a roll call of future revolutionaries. These men returned to Saint Domingue with military experience and a new sense of their own importance. Prominent free coloreds secretly drew up a report attacking the caste system and in 1784 sent a representative to France.[6]

The revolt in Saint-Domingue that ultimately led to an independent Haitian nation began with a slave uprising in the northern province of the country. While the precise date is often cited as August 22, 1791, the date of the Bois Caïman Voodoo ceremony[7], other scholars see an earlier organization and planning meeting as the true birthday of the Haitian Revolution.

On Sunday, August 14th, a meeting of slave-drivers, coachmen, and other members of the "slave elite" from about 100 plantations took place in Plaine du Nord parish. They gathered on the Lenormand de Mézy estate, a large sugar cane plantation with at least 350 slaves that lay at the foot of the Red Mountain. After discussions of political developments in France and the colony, they took the decision to rebel.[8]

Prior to the 1791 slave uprising, Saint-Domingue was known as one of the quietest of the Caribbean colonies. This was indeed remarkable considering its large slave population. *In all, Dominguan colonists bought approximately 800,000 Africans, nearly as many as the total*

___
6  David Patrick Geggus, *Haitian Revolutionary Studies* (Bloomington, IL: Indiana University Press, 2002), 8. This regiment (Chasseurs-Volontaires de Saint-Domingue) suffered heavy casualties against the British forces in the battle of Savannah, Georgia in 1779.

7  The Bois Caïman ceremony is discussed in chapter VII, Mission Challenge: Voodoo and Catholicism in Haiti, 57.

8  Geggus, *Haitian Revolutionary Studies*, 84 – 85.

*slave imports of Britain's 13 North American colonies combined.*[9] And yet once the revolt in the north took hold, spread to other provinces of the colony, and acquired the leaders later revered by patriotic Haitians, it became the most successful slave uprising in late 18th – early 19th century. The revolt of 1791 would lead ultimately in 1804 to the declaration of an independent nation, primarily composed of former slaves.

From 1793 to 1802, the most renowned and feared leader of the Saint-Domingue uprising was Toussaint L'Ouverture[10] (François-Domenica Bréda). He is now regarded as the George Washington, or founding father of the nation of Haiti. While a French commissar, Léger-Félicité Sonthonax, sent to regain control of the colony *was forced to declare free all slaves willing to fight under the French republican flag, in August 1793 Toussaint Louverture raised the stakes with his proclamation from Camp Turel: immediate unconditional freedom and equality for all.*[11] L'Ouverture managed to gain control of then Spanish-held Santo Domingo, which occupied the other two-thirds of the island of Hispaniola. However, the great strategist of the Haitian revolution was eventually tricked into meeting with the French general Charles Leclerc (brother-in-law to Napoleon Bonaparte) on the pretext of negotiating a settlement to the conflict. He was arrested by force and packed off to France where he would later die in April of 1803.

Toussaint L'Ouverture was joined in the revolt by a host of now famous revolutionaries and generals — some of whom later became kings, emperors, or presidents of the new nation. These included Jean-Jacques Dessalines, and Henri Christophe. Control of the Haitian army passed from L'Ouverture to Dessalines with the former's extradition to France. Dessalines overwhelmingly defeated the French forces under Leclerc's

---

9    John D. Garrigus, "The Legacies of Pre-revolutionary Saint-Domingue," in *Haiti Rising: Haitian History, Culture and the Earthquake of 2010*, Martin Munro, ed. (Kingston, Jamaica: University of the West Indies Press, 2010), 118.
10   Toussaint L'Ouverture is memorialized on Haitian currency, in art and literature, and his name was given to the primary entry point for travelers into the country — the international airport just north of the capitol, Port-au-Prince.
11   Michel-Rolph Trouillot, "An Unthinkable History: The Haitian Revolution as a Non-Event," in *Haitian History: New Perspectives*, Alyssa Goldstein Sepinwall, ed. (New York, NY: Routledge, 2013), 43.

replacement, the vicomte de Rochembeau, at the Battle of Vertières in November of 1803. It was Dessalines who chose to name the new country Haiti, from the Taíno word *ayiti* meaning "land of mountains." He declared the country's independence from Napoleon's France on January 1, 1804.

Haiti's newly won independence was at first not recognized by the major powers — especially the former colonial overlord France. In 1825, some twenty-one years after Dessalines declared Haiti free and independent, an agreement was reached in which the government of Haiti agreed to pay an indemnity to France of 150 million gold francs. In exchange, the government of France formally recognized Haiti's independence and lifted its trade embargo. Some years later, the indemnity was later reduced to a sum of 90 million francs. But because the Haitian government was forced to borrow the money at exorbitant interest rates from banks in order to pay the indemnity, it remained a drain on the Haitian economy until the debt was retired in 1947. Some of the current revenue problems of the country and its foreign debt can be traced back to this original French indemnity.

The period from 1804 to the 1890s is often hailed by Haitian scholars and specialists as the golden age of the nation's history. Between 1805 and 1820 one of the proudest landmarks in Haitian history was constructed by military strategist Henri Christophe. The Citadelle Laferrière, designed to deter a possible French invasion, is a massive fortress built near Cap-Haïtien and is one of the recognized symbols of the Haitian nation. During most of the 19th century, despite the ongoing debt payments to France, Haiti enjoyed the fruits of its independence. *Because of the country's size and political independence, former slaves were able to establish themselves as peasant farmers, unlike newly freed people in many other Caribbean colonies, where colonial planters retained control of the land after slavery.*[12] While this growth in population and the proliferation of small family farming plots sustained its internal stability through the days of leaders like Alexandre Pétion (1806 – 1820), Jean Pierre Boyer (1820 – 1843) and President Faustin Soulouque (1849 – 1859), these two factors would also contribute to

12  Garrigus, "The Legacies of Pre-revolutionary Saint-Domingue," 118.

Haiti's twin 21$^{st}$ century problems of overpopulation and inability to feed itself. As Garrigus observes:

> By 1918 the population had reached an estimated 1.9 million, up from roughly half a million in 1790. Over the course of the twentieth century the country's population quadrupled again, growing to an estimated nine million today. The kind of agriculture that made Haiti a peasant's paradise in the 1800s cannot support the many millions more families that have been added over the last hundred years.[13]

During the 1820s to 1840s, problems that still exist between Haiti and its Dominican Republic neighbor began with the Haitian occupation of the Spanish two-thirds of the island during the presidency of Jean Boyer. The colony of Santo Domingo had declared its independence from Spain and originally explored joining Simón Bolívar's movement in South America. However, some powerful interests in Santo Domingo encouraged Boyer to occupy the newly freed former colony. The Haitian government ruled the Dominicans harshly and helped encourage a revolt which successfully put an end to Haiti's dominance over her larger neighbor. The Dominican resentment, however, remains always in the background, impacting the relationship between these two countries.

The mid to late 20$^{th}$ century pattern of totalitarian regimes and the sometimes violent overthrow of the nation's leaders is another pattern that is easily detected in the previous period of the early 19$^{th}$ century through 1915. Even in cases in which the emperor, king, or president of Haiti governed for some time with success, the transfer of power to the next regime seldom occurred peacefully. And this tendency to abrupt changes in government reached its unstable peak in the years 1911 – 1915. In this five-year period prior to the major U.S. occupation of the country, no less than seven administrations governed Haiti.[14] Some of these presidents were murdered, while others were exiled.

Another of the major historical events that have shaped Haiti is the

---

13  Ibid., 118.
14  Patrick Belgarde-Smith, "Uprisings, Insurrections, and Political Movements: Contemporary Haiti and the Teachings of History, 1957 – 2010," in *Haiti Rising: Haitian History, Culture and the Earthquake of 2010*, Martin Munro, ed. (Kingston, Jamaica: University of the West Indies Press, 2010), 137.

U.S. occupation of the country from 1915 to 1934. There were many factors that pushed the United States into taking direct action in Haiti. Many scholars point out that these were the years of tension preceding the First World War. German economic interests and influence had been growing in Haiti prior to 1915. German bankers were in possession of many of the high-interest loans the country had taken on in order to make its debt payments to France. And in fact the Germans in Haiti controlled a disproportionate amount of the banking, transportation, and other economic sectors. This was after all an era in America's own national history in which it was committed to eliminating European exercises of power in the Western Hemisphere and promotion of its own hegemony and economic interests. However, it was the extreme instability of Haiti's many governments during these years, and the violence with which one succeeded another, that brought American troops into the nation.

Opinions vary as to the relative benefits versus the harm done to the nation during the period. However, an undeniable fact remains that the American policies encouraged the resettlement of farmers into Port-au-Prince[15], exploding the city and creating what is today a virtually unsustainable density of people. And whereas prior to the American invasion there had been at least five thriving coastal cities, each with successful port facilities, Port-au-Prince was somewhat artificially designated as the preferred point of import and export for commodities.

Meanwhile, the United States Marines, in an effort to control revolutionary movements in the rural areas, built a useful road system, but also left a well-trained and politically-active national army, the *Garde d'Haïti* — an institution that would factor heavily in Haitian politics for much of the remainder of the 20th century. While the Haitian fascination with the United States no doubt began long before this period, it was during the American occupation that a mixed perception of the U.S. began to form in the Haitian national conscience. Most Haitians today love American tourists and missionaries, yet look with great suspicion and doubt upon the actions of its government with respect to Haiti's

15 This was a crucial component of U.S. strategy designed to weaken the 'rebellious' power base headquartered in the northern province in Cap-Haïtien.

own national interests. With a cursory knowledge of the period of the American occupation and its detrimental lingering effects one can see why Haitians hold such a 'mixed' perspective on the United States. As Alyssa Goldstein Sepinwall writes:

> The U.S. exit in 1934 left Haiti with what appeared to be a second independence, a chance to begin again. However, as in other modern decolonizations, even when the United States departed, it did not stop trying to intervene in Haitian affairs. Though ground forces disappeared, efforts to profit from Haiti continued. U.S. banks still controlled Haiti's financial system, and U.S. companies obtained monopoly rights for industries such as rubber and bananas, on land that had been cultivated by subsistence farmers. Haitian President Sténio Vincent, who had been a noted anti-occupation leader, transformed into a close ally of the U.S. He continued the transformation of the Haitian military that had begun under the Marines. Whereas in the nineteenth century, the army had been intended as a bulwark against foreign invasion, the newly professionalized Haitian army became a powerful institution designed to crush domestic opposition.[16]

During the first administration of President Franklin Roosevelt, under the umbrella of his Good Neighbor policy, the U.S. withdrew from Haiti in 1934. While the occupying troops were no longer in the country, America continued to manage Haiti's international finances until the French indemnity was retired in 1947. By the end of the American occupation, the rising class of black professionals working in the country were shifting in their sympathies from the old French ways toward the cultural heritage transmitted through their African ancestors. And it was during this period that Dr. François Duvalier became an advocate for this African shift in Haitian consciousness as the editor of the publication *Les Griots*. Duvalier was soon to make a much deeper impact on his country than that which could be accomplished with a pen and a printing press.

Sténio Vincent won the 1930 election in Haiti and became its president during the period of American withdrawal and the restoration of

---

16 Alyssa Goldstein Sepinwall, "From the Occupation to the Earthquake: Haiti in the Twentieth and Twenty-First Centuries," in *Haitian History: New Perspectives*, Alyssa Goldstein Sepinwall, ed. (New York, NY: Routledge Press, 2013), 217 – 218.

Haitian sovereignty over its own national affairs. What began with the promise of a better future for the country, however, quickly moved in the direction of totalitarianism — a totalitarianism that was more absolute than in the 19<sup>th</sup> century, because Vincent enjoyed the advantage of the unified *Garde d'Haïti*. In 1935, Vincent manipulated the legislature into approving a new constitution that granted him virtually dictatorial powers. Haiti's brief flirtation with a genuine democracy came to a hasty end as it reverted to the strongman style of executive leadership which had marked many of its 19<sup>th</sup> century governments.

The old tensions between Haiti and the Dominican Republic were dramatically heightened during the days of the Vincent regime. But this time, the conflict was not Haitian in origin. Rafael Leónidas Trujillo Molina, the dictator of the Dominican Republic during this era, had plans for gaining control of his Haitian neighbor. While seeking to influence the Haitian army through bribery, he also ordered the murder of an estimated 15,000 to 20,000 Haitians living just inside Dominican territory along the Massacre River. This bloody and barbarous act, carried out by the Dominican army in October of 1937, further fueled the century-old animosity between these two island-sharing nations.

Vincent's administration was followed by that of his hand-picked successor, Antoine Louis Léocardie Élie Lescot, who governed from 1941 until the beginning of 1946. Lescot, like Vincent, was an authoritarian ruler and became so unpopular with certain segments of Haitian society that he was forced to resign January 11, 1946 in the wake of rising strikes and protests in some of the major cities. Lescot by that time had also lost the support of the Garde d'Haïti and thus could not maintain his grip on the reins of power.

The Revolution of 1946 is viewed by many as a new development in Haiti's long history. It is not unusual at all that the Élie Lescot government was toppled, but rather that it was forced out through a combination of popular strikes and the direct involvement of the Haitian army. And from 1946 until the dismantling of the Haitian army, the military played a significant role in the political landscape of Haiti. The eventual result of the 1946 revolution and the political maneuvering that went on between the rival factions and the military was the victory of Dumarsais Estimé, a modest school teacher, as the next president of Haiti. Estimé was forced out of office by the military in May 1950, in reaction to reforms he was attempting to make which were unpopular with Haiti's elite and mulatto populations. There are many older Haitians in the country today who will strongly argue that Dumarsais Estimé was the last effective president the country enjoyed — that in those days Haiti was a much better and more prosperous nation. Estimé raised the status of the army, in March 1947 renaming it the *Armée d'Haïti*. It was members of the new *Armée d'Haïti* who conveyed him into exile in Jamaica.

Estimé was succeeded by Paul E. Magloire, who enjoyed the support of the elites and the military, and won the national elections in October 1950. This was an era of mixed outcomes for Haiti's economy, a tourist boom was going on in Port-au-Prince, but severe economic hardships were the norm for those living in the outlying rural areas.

> Port-au-Prince enjoyed something of a golden age in the 1950s. The city became a Caribbean hot spot that competed for tourists with Havana and San Juan. It boasted fountained tropical plazas, gleaming Beaux-Arts buildings, and an International Casino pier where glass-bottomed boats set out for tours of a coral reef. ... Yet on the margins of the capitol and in the countryside were signs of an economy on the brink. Overpopulation, deforestation, and a decline in crop prices — particularly coffee — were driving down agricultural production.[17]

Like many before him, Magloire sought to exceed the elected term of his office and refused to step down. The truth is that the Haitian presidency is typically seen as a doorway to great riches and it with great reluctance that the powerful office and its perks are laid aside. Like Lescot and Estimé before him, Magloire was forced out of office into exile in Jamaica through a general strike in May of 1956 and pressure from the military. Perhaps Magloire's most significant legacy to Haiti was the chaotic period which ensued upon his removal from office. Between May of 1956 and September of 1957, three different administrations attempted to govern the nation of Haiti. And this highly erratic period would give

---

17 Jonathan M. Katz, *The Big Truck That Went By: How the World Came to Save Haiti and Left Behind a Disaster* (New York, NY: Palgrave Macmillan, 2013), 42.

rise to perhaps the most dominant rulers in Haitian history since the early 1800s—the father and son known as Papa and Baby Doc.

In the fall of 1957, Dr. François Duvalier, minister for health under a previous administration, handily won the national election held after a more than one year of unstable governments. Thus began a remarkable period of some 30 years of control by François Duvalier and his son Jean-Claude. During the period, the Duvaliers ruled through fear, intimidation, superstition, and their own sort of private army. Duvalier was a *Vodouisant*, or Voodoo adherent, and was rumored to be involved in magic and sorcery connected with the religion.

The Haitian people today bear the scars and a sort of collective, national memory of the Duvalier era. One can often elicit a flood of emotions and stories by asking an older Haitian about the *Tontons Macoutes*[18], the Duvalier regime's paramilitary police. The so-called *Volontaires de la Sécurité Nationale* (Volunteers for National Security), later renamed the *Milice de Volontaires de la Sécurité Nationale* (Militia of National Security Volunteers) served the Duvaliers loyally and ruthlessly. The rural populations at first were grateful for Duvalier and he knew precisely how to engender that loyalty:

> One of the methods Duvalier used to recruit support in rural areas and to maintain control throughout the country was by developing the organisation of *tontons macoutes*. 'Excellency,' declared one *macoute* leader in 1960, addressing the president, 'the gun that Sonthonax gave us to defend our liberty and that the American occupation has taken away from us is the gun that, without fear, you have restored to us—be assured that this gun will not be used against you.[19]

---

18 *Perhaps the most notorious feature of Haiti under the Duvaliers has been the militia, popularly known as the tontons macoutes (after the figure in Haitian folklore who carries off wicked children in his bag). The organization originated as a private paramilitary group during the election of 1956-7.* David Nicholls, "Rural Protest and Peasant Revolt, 1804 – 1869," in *Haitian History: New Perspectives*, Alyssa Goldstein Sepinwall, ed. (New York, NY: Routledge Press, 2013), 180. Since the days of the U.S. occupation, especially after a revolt in 1919 was put down, the majority of Haitian people had been unarmed. Duvalier rearmed the masses to support his regime.

19 David Nicholls, "Rural Protest and Peasant Revolt, 1804 – 1869," 193.

While the records of the era are not complete it is estimated that some 30,000 Haitian people were killed during Papa Doc's rule of the country. His *Tontons Macoutes* also routinely intimidated, brutally beat, raped, or imprisoned political opponents. They propped-up and defended the regime's friends at home while encouraging Duvalier's opponents to flee the country. Their influence continued even after Duvalier's son Baby Doc was removed from power.

François Duvalier died in April of 1971 and his power passed down to his then nineteen-year-old son Jean-Claude, known to Haitians as Baby Doc. The elder Duvalier had changed the 1964 Constitution in order for his son to be eligible for the presidency. Laurent Dubois writes about the initial results of his ascension to power:

> The younger Duvalier was widely considered a protected playboy lacking the political skills of his father, and many thought that his reign would not last long. But despite a series of family dramas that intrigued and entertained many observers, he would stay in power for fourteen years. It helped, of course, that he inherited his father's well-established system of control and extraction, as well as close ties with the U.S. administration. During his time in office, Haiti's relationship with the United States and other countries continued to improve, and an increasing amount of foreign investment began coming into the country. Corporations eager to take advantage of the low cost of labor in Haiti built factories to produce wigs, clothes, and baseballs. There was some incongruity to the last item, since Haitians themselves never took up the American sport. Soon, however, every baseball used in the U.S. professional leagues was made in Haiti.[20]

For some years under the younger ruler, the lot of the Haitian people seemed to be slowly improving. Economic development appeared to be moving in an upward direction. Duvalier also enjoyed some political popularity. But this was not to last. For after this early Baby Doc era of growing economic investment in Haiti and the equivalent of three billion dollars in today's money in largely U.S. aid, the situation in Haiti began to grow more unstable again.

---

20  Laurent Dubois, *Haiti: The Aftershocks of History* (New York: New York: Metropolitan Books, 2012), 350.

The younger Duvalier and his family lived a garishly lavish life-style and apparently skimmed large quantities of U.S. aid money from the Haitian treasury into his own Swiss accounts.[21] His wife Michèle Bennett threw lavish parties in the early 1980s and one particularly notorious soirée at Christmastime was televised for the Haitian people. Eventually three anti-Duvalier protestors in November of 1985 were shot in Gonaïves. This sparked student protests and even condemnation from the Voodoo community. Jean-Claude Duvalier was removed from power and sent into exile—the way of so many Haitian presidents—on February 7, 1986. How do historians and economists view the Duvalier era's impact on Haiti? Jean-Germain Gros summarizes the Duvaliers as adding to Haiti's misery and its failure as a viable state:

> In sum, there are no substantive differences between François Duvalier and Jean-Claude Duvalier. They governed the same way with nearly identical results. Haiti was a failed state in 1957, when François Duvalier took over, and a failed state when Jean-Claude Duvalier left in 1986. That both Duvaliers kept a semblance of order in Haiti in no way connotes that Haiti was a strong state. The failed state is, once again, a state that is severely incapac-itated when it comes to the basic functions of statecraft. It is

---

21 *Throughout their tenures, the Duvaliers cynically promoted the idea of Haiti as a diseased polity that demanded rapid infusions of international aid. They appealed to every imaginable source of aid, but especially to USAID, which some in Haiti have termed "a state within a state." The Duvaliers also turned to Canada, France, West Germany, and to the World Bank and International Monetary Fund, to UNICEF and the United Nations Development Program, and to the World Health Organization. One recent study estimated that, during the 1970s and 1980s, such aid financed two-thirds of government investment and covered fully half of Haitian import expenditures. Despite obvious evidence of massive fraud, these organizations happily pumped money into the Duvalier kleptocracy: While AID was being so charmingly credulous, the US Department of Commerce produced figures to show that no less than 63 per cent of all recorded government revenue in Haiti was being "misappropriated" each year. Not long afterwards – and just before he was dismissed by Duvalier – Haiti's Finance Minister, Marc Bazin, revealed that a monthly average of $15 million was being diverted from public funds to meet "extra-budgetary expenses" that included regular deposits into the President's private Swiss bank account. Most of these "public funds" had, of course, arrived in Haiti in the form of "development assistance."* Paul Farmer, *The Uses of Haiti* (Monroe, MA: Common Courage Press, 3rd ed. 2006), 290 – 291.

also a state where power is extremely insecure, which generates behavior patterns tending toward personal rule, despotism, even paranoia. Did these conditions obtain in Duvalier-ruled Haiti? The evidence is overwhelming.[22]

The economic and human consequences to the nation of Haiti from the Duvalier dynasty were horrendous. The infusion of American capital and the appearance of order and stability (which the Tontons Macoutes maintained by fear and intimidation) masked an emasculated nation. Dubois' assessment of the Duvalier legacy is quite bleak:

> The thirty years of Duvalier rule left behind a devastated country. As many as a million Haitians had fled into exile. The treasury was empty. The civil institutions that had previously provided an alternative means of organizing Haitian society had been largely demolished of absorbed by the state. Haiti was still burdened by crushing foreign debt and battered by foreign involvement in affairs. And while international investment and aid had helped to build up some aspects of the country's infrastructure, what remained of the state had little capacity to maintain it. The only truly functioning institution that Duvalier left behind was a massive military apparatus.[23]

Another question that must be raised, especially by anyone seeking to enter the Haitian culture as a missionary, is this: "How has the United States contributed, either knowingly or unintentionally, to Haiti's present misery?" Clearly America bears its share of responsibility, especially during the long occupation early in the 20th century, for the mass resettlement and overcrowding of the Haitian people into the Port-au-Prince metropolitan area. And the U.S. cannot escape responsibility for helping sustain the Duvaliers in power, at least until Baby Doc's administration

---

22   Jean-Germain Gros, *State Failure, Underdevelopment, and Foreign Intervention in Haiti* (New York, NY: Routledge, 2012), 116 – 117. In the same work, Gros demonstrates through analysis of Haitian military expenditures during the period that as he writes, *The Duvalierist state further underdeveloped Haiti through its security policy, the aim of which was predominantly regime security. He adds, It is not implausible that at the heights of the crisis of Duvalierism (1959 – 63) spending on the Tontons Macoutes might have even outstripped spending on the regular army* (see pages 118 – 119).
23   Laurent Dubois, *Haiti: The Aftershocks of History*, 358.

finally proved itself unable to stabilize the country 1986. Perhaps the somewhat leftist assessment of Patrick Belgarde-Smith concerning American government involvement in Haiti between 1915 and 1986 and its consequences are not far from an accurate critique:

> Political stability for economic growth, rather than development, had been the leitmotiv of American plans for Haiti. Social justice was never an issue. A non-ambitious plan for enclave export assembly industries was to be Haiti's salvation, according to American economists. The agricultural sector would be decimated, both in production and its labor, to sustain the urban industries. But the world's cheapest workforce did little for rapidly underdeveloping Haiti. Schemes for Haitian development increased Haitian poverty. There were uprisings, small-scale invasions from abroad, passive resistance, and large migrations abroad, both from professional ranks and later from impoverished peasants and urban workers. The Haitian diaspora is one of the largest in the world.[24]

The political situation in Haiti was again chaotic with Baby Doc's departure from power. And as was previously noted the economic conditions faced by the majority of Haitians had worsened, rather than improved. *Less than 1 percent of Haitians receive about 44 percent of all income, but pay only 3.5 percent of taxes, the leaving the overburdened majority with the rest of the bill.*[25] During the transition period between Jean-Claude Duvalier and the next president, Jean-Bertrand Aristide, Haiti adopted the new Constitution of 1987, which sought to decrease centralized power, legalized the practice of Voodoo, elevated Haitian Creole to an official language status, and removed Roman Catholicism as the state religion. Yet the climate of instability, political maneuvering, and *death and mayhem at the hands of the army and the remnants of the Duvalierist Macoutes*[26] continued. This period witnessed, as in an earlier period, some seven governments within a four year period. As Belgarde-Smith explains:

---

24 Patrick Belgarde-Smith, "Uprisings, Insurrections, and Political Movements: Contemporary Haiti and the Teachings of History, 1957 – 2010," 138.
25 Ibid., 138.
26 Ibid., 141.

A number of provisional military governments took over after consultation with the United States. In February 1988 in flawed elections, Professor Leslie F. Manigat was named president for a five-year term that lasted only five months. The army deposed Manigat, and ruled again directly. ... There were coup d'état within coup d'état, inside the army itself, when one general would replace another, then another. ... General Henri Namphy resigned the presidency; General Prosper Avril also resigned as president; General Hérard Abraham resigned as president to hand over power to Madame Ertha Pascal-Trouillot, the first woman judge at the Cour de Cassation, Haiti's supreme court, ... Her sole function was to give the country fair elections, which resulted in Jean-Bertrand Aristide attaining the presidency for a period of five years that ended a mere seven months later in September 1991.[27]

Aristide was a man of socialist leanings and enjoyed the favor of then French President François Maurice Mitterrand. He was therefore considered to be a dangerous threat to the elite and to the middle class of professionals and government employees. His political leanings also put him at odds with the Catholic Church, Haitian business leaders, and the United States government. Aristide was forced out of power in September 1991 by an internal military coup. He was later returned to power through diplomatic pressure from the Clinton Administration and the very real threat of U.S. military intervention. In the elections of 1995, Aristide was able to put forward a political friend and ally, René G. Préval, who was elected Haiti's next president. Préval took office in February of 1996 in a ceremony noteworthy as the first orderly transition between two democratically elected Haitian presidents.

Aristide returned to power as Haiti's president through the disputed elections of November 2000. Many eligible voters and opposition groups boycotted the national election. A rising tide of allegations of drug trafficking against the president and his inner circle, coupled with continued opposition from key sectors of the country helped spark a revolt in 2004. Eventually the key city of Gonaïves came under full rebel control. As forces began marching on Port-au-Prince, it is generally believed that

---

27  Patrick Belgarde-Smith, "Uprisings, Insurrections, and Political Movements: Contemporary Haiti and the Teachings of History, 1957 – 2010," 141.

U.S. officials and former Haitian military leaders forced Aristide to resign and to enter exile in Africa. Aristide's socialistic tendencies were viewed as a threat by the Americans and his disbanding of the Haitian army made him a persona non grata with the officer class.

There remain today very strong opinions among Haitians concerning the Aristide era, even as the Duvaliers period continues to influence perspectives among the middle-aged and older generations. For the majority of Haitians at the bottom end of the economic structures, Aristide remains a hero and his administration is remembered as a more joyful time for Haiti. As recently as May 2013 Aristide was summoned to appear in court in Port-au-Prince. He chose deliberately to walk to the courthouse on foot. Hundreds of thousands of poor Haitians gathered together from villages and suburbs of the capitol and descended upon the courthouse area, bringing downtown Port-au-Prince to a standstill, in support of their former president, who in their eyes remains a popular leftist hero of the downtrodden.

In May of 2006, René Préval was elected to fulfill a second term as president of Haiti. His second presidential term was marked by escalating food prices which sparked protests in 2008, the year which also saw four severe hurricanes (Fay, Gustav, Hanna, and Ike) which added to the difficulties and suffering of the Haitian people. The last year of Préval's presidency was occupied with the relief and recovery efforts demanded by the devastating January 2010 earthquake, aftershocks, and related cholera epidemic. His reluctance to rally the Haitian nation through public speeches or through the press apparatus led to increasing dissatisfaction with his administration.

The current president of Haiti, Michel Martelly, otherwise known as "Sweet Micky"[28], was elected in a run-off election on April 4, 2011. While his initial assumption of office was greeted by great enthusiasm and anticipation by a large portion of Haiti's impoverished people, there has been little improvement in infrastructure, availability of food, economic

---

28  Michael Martelly was an extremely popular entertainer on the Haitian music scene prior to his campaign for the presidency of Haiti. As of November 2013 his popularity is in decline over lack of progress in the nation's recovery and in economic growth.

growth, or increase in the standard of living. As missionaries return to Haiti in 2013, they find more and more Haitians deeply disillusioned with the Martelly administration.

And in a sort of proof of the cyclical theory of history — at least Haitian history at any rate — both Jean-Claude Duvalier and Jean-Bertrand Aristide have returned from exile to the country they once ruled. And they both continue to exercise great power behind the scenes in the Haitian political landscape. *Duvalier's son and Papa Doc's grandson, a 29-year-old Francois Nicolas Duvalier, is a consultant to President Martelly.*[29]

## Conclusion

This brief summary of the long and tumultuous history of Haiti demonstrates how very necessary it is for incoming missionaries to possess some basic knowledge about how God has prepared Haiti for the Gospel. The complexity of Haiti's present culture and the kaleidoscope of its people's perspectives are the mature fruit of its history and that history's impact upon their families, their farms, their cities, and their political institutions. What the missionary sees when engaged with the people and places of Haiti need not perplex them. They need only to embrace an understanding of God's providence at work in Haitian history — to understand that much as the psalmist declares in Psalm 102:13, *You will arise and have pity on Zion; it is the time to favor her; the appointed time has come. For your servants hold her stones dear and have pity on her dust.*

The patterns of unstable and ineffective governments in Haiti reach back to the early 20th century and the years of crisis in 1911 to 1915. And the sometimes chaotic and brutal transitions from one Haitian government to the next are nothing new to this 21st century either. In fact, for

---

29  Jonathan M. Katz, *The Big Truck That Went By: How the World Came to Save Haiti and Left Behind a Disaster* (New York, NY: Palgrave Macmillan, 2013), 282. Katz also notes that, "In January of 2012, a Haitian judge ruled that Jean-Claude 'Baby Doc' Duvalier could not be prosecuted for the innumerable human-rights abuses of his reign; flouting protests from Human Rights Watch and Amnesty International, the judge found that the statute of limitations on crimes in the indictment had expired."

much of Haiti's two hundred years of independence it has been this way. Haiti's government has always struggled to maintain an atmosphere of stability, free-enterprise, and emergency management. Jean-Germaine Gros rather despairingly writes:

> As it is conventionally understood, that state has never existed in Haiti. Yet, the state is condition sine qua non for the prosperity of nations. The root cause of Haitian poverty is, therefore, the absence of a working state. Haiti is also a country that is 80 percent mountains. All of its major cities are seaside agglomerations, which make them vulnerable to hurricanes, floods, and mudslides, not to mention the threat of foreign invasion. The population has grown from half a million to nearly 10 million in the past 215 years. Meanwhile, the technology of production, especially as it relates to agriculture, has barely changed since the demise of colonialism because the insecurity of property rights wrought, once again, by a dysfunctional state acts as a disincentive to innovation. Moreover, the inability of the Haitian state to insure against risks increases transaction costs, which have deleterious consequences on the efficiency of exchange and by extension the economy.[30]

And for those who are quick to assume that the United States should just "come in and fix the country," it must be said that official U.S. involvement at many times in Haiti's history has often done far more harm than good. American governments have made some poor choices at times with reference to the Haitian administrations they have supported with both dollars and destroyers.

Some first-timers to Haiti are struck by the seeming dependency of many Haitians upon charitable hand-outs in order to survive. They question the 'lack of initiative' and they marvel at the poverty so unavoidably obvious to even the casual observer. Yet these deep scars upon the beautiful faces of the people of Haiti are partly the result of a very unhealthy co-dependency — a co-dependency developed over many decades of foreign intervention, and foreign tampering, and yes, foreign charity in Haiti.

---

30  Jean-Germain Gros, *State Failure, Underdevelopment, and Foreign Intervention in Haiti* (New York, NY: Routledge, 2012), XIV.

For Americans visiting Haiti it is important to also understand the deep connections that have been created between the U.S. and Haiti through expatriate Haitians. Many of them have pursued a widely-held aspiration among their countrymen — to create a new life for themselves in places like Miami, New York, or Atlanta. As Jonathan Katz observes, *Haitian Americans have prospered and play major roles in American life while sustaining millions on the island with money sent back (remittances make up more than a quarter of the Haitian economy).*[31]

With all of this Haitian historical story beneath the surface in mind, the missionary will be able to more accurately appreciate what God has been doing to bring Haiti to the doorstep of the kingdom, and to properly exegete[32] Haitian culture and Haitian people in order to better show them the riches found only in Christ.

---

31  Jonathan M. Katz, *The Big Truck That Went By: How the World Came to Save Haiti and Left Behind a Disaster* (New York, NY: Palgrave Macmillan, 2013), 3.

32  The term exegete comes from the word exegesis, which means the process of carefully study, analysis, and then interpretation of a text from Scripture. To exegete Haitian culture involves the study, analysis, and then the drawing of conclusions in order to help the missionary to interact and engage with the Haitian people.

*This derelect facility in the Port-au-Prince area represents a once more prosperous, yet American-involved Haiti. It was the primary sugar cane processing plant owned by the Haitian-American Sugar Cane Company (HASCO). HASCO ceased active operation in 1987, with the loss of more than 35,000 jobs.*

*Pastor Jean Jacob Paul, the Haitian-American God called to return to his native Haiti and spread the Gospel of Jesus Christ.*

*And a vision appeared to Paul in the night: a man*
*of Macedonia was standing there, urging him and*
*saying, "Come over to Macedonia and help us." And*
*when Paul had seen the vision, immediately we sought*
*to go on into Macedonia, concluding that God had*
*called us to preach the gospel to them.*
*(Acts 16:9 – 10)*

# CHAPTER II
# Mission Calling: God Returns
# An American Citizen to Haiti

Jean Jacob Paul tried again and again to stop the new SUV as it spun round and round across the steel tracks of the railroad crossing. His wife Jocelyne realized with horror that the distant sound, growing louder and louder was a freight train, barreling toward the crossing. As the seconds raced by, unable to jump from the spinning machine, they braced themselves for a life-ending collision. And then, just as abruptly as the SUV's swirling had begun, it stopped. Jean immediately slammed the gas pedal to the floor and their shiny new car cleared the train tracks with only seconds to spare. In their rearview mirror, they could see the massive locomotive moving across the very spot on the tracks where they had been trapped just seconds before.

Earlier that Christmas Eve morning, they had picked-up the new Mitsubishi Montero at an Atlanta showroom as a Christmas present for the family. What in the world had just happened? Jean knew one thing for certain, he was not taking his family to Callaway Gardens for a holiday in that crazy SUV. When Jean and Jocelyne arrived safely home, he told the children they would leave for Christmas break in the morning, after he had returned that dangerous vehicle.

That night, as Jean slept, he encountered a familiar person in an all-too-familiar dream. An older man, dressed in a white shirt and navy pants, appeared before him and said, "Jean, the only reason I did not take your life today at the railroad crossing was because your wife was in the car with you. Are you finally going to go to Haiti or am I going to take you to Haiti?"

Just as the man was finished speaking, Jean felt as though he was being shaken by a pair of hands. He woke up to find that Jocelyne was extremely upset and trying to get his attention. She said, "I just had a very strange dream. A man dressed in a white shirt and navy pants appeared before me and said that he was going to take your life today at the railroad crossing, but didn't do it because I was with you." What in the world is this all about Jean? Jean started to explain everything that God had been doing in his life up to that very night — things he had never told Jocelyne before or after they got married.

Jean Jacob Paul's father died when Jean was only three years old. But it would not be long before God began revealing his calling upon the young Jean, doing so when he was a small boy of eight, living in very primitive conditions. Jean walked into an evangelistic tent meeting near his Haitian village. As he strained to see the missionary preaching way up front, the evangelist, a Canadian called to bring the Gospel to Haiti, began explaining that the Lord had told him that one of the young boys packed into that very service had a special calling of God on his life.

As the Canadian preacher continued, Jean watched the man's assistant moving from row to row, pointing at this boy or that boy and waiting for the evangelist to nod his head. On and on the assistant went picking boy after boy and moving further and further back into the crowded tent. All the while the preacher was shaking his head 'no' and urging his assistant to keep going.

And then to Jean's surprise the assistant pointed to him and to his amazement the preacher way down front exclaimed, "That's the boy God has called!" The man brought Jean through the crowd and up to the front of the meeting. The preacher looked at him and said, "God has called you to bring the Good News of Jesus Christ to the people of Haiti. I am going to take you to the United States, see that you get trained in the Bible, and then you will come back here and tell the people about Jesus!"

How does a boy delivered from a place of abject misery by the hand of God find himself returned to that same place as a man preaching the Gospel? The simple answer of course is found in the amazing providence of God. Yet the story of Jean Jacob Paul's dramatic 'last call' through an urgent dream demonstrates how unique the calling of God truly is for each of his redeemed children.

Jean Paul was taken from Haiti in 1968 and placed with a Caucasian family in New York City. His foster mother, Mrs. Williams, became as dear to Jean as his birth mother in Haiti. He was also close to Mrs. William's two sons. Growing up Jean had as many white friends as African-American. He enjoyed America's promise and her prosperity.

Jean studied the Bible at Morris Cerullo School of Ministry in California and graduated just as had been planned and expected of him. From his arrival in the United States in 1968 until his graduation from Bible college, Jean had been supported by the mission organization which had brought him from Haiti to Mrs. William's home.

On the day of Jean's graduation, an elderly man with a cane walked slowly toward him. The man asked Jean, "Do you know who I am son? I am so proud of you today and so thankful to God." Jean replied, "No sir. I have no idea who you are. Should I know you?" The old man explained, "I am Dan Alexis, the missionary who was preaching the service in Haiti when God called you to learn the Bible and preach the Gospel to the people of Haiti."

The retired missionary then handed Jean a graduation card and an envelope that contained one thousand dollars in cash. He said, "Congratulations! Now you can return to Haiti and fulfill God's calling on your life — to preach the truth about the Lord Jesus to those who live in darkness there." Jean thanked the kindly old man whom God had used so carefully to bring him to that day. But Jean did not tell Mr. Alexis what he really planned to do next. Jean had no intention of returning to Haiti. Instead, Jean used the missionary's graduation money to buy a plane ticket back to New York, not Port-au-Prince. Once back in the Big Apple, Jean pursued his own plan instead of the one God had set before him. Jean wanted to be an engineer, not a minister of the Gospel.

When Jean finished telling his story of how the Lord had been working in his life since he was a child, Jocelyne exclaimed, "Well then you must go to Haiti. I would rather have you alive and far away in Haiti than bury you here in America!"

Even as Jean began to hide from God's calling upon his life, not unlike the prophet Jonah, so also God used all Jean's time of resisting to prepare him for the day when Jean would finally yield. And like the prophet Jonah, Jean finally learned that you cannot hide from God, or escape his purpose for your life. That day finally came on Christmas Eve 2002.

By the time Jean Paul arrived in Port-au-Prince on October 31, 2003, he had been made ready by God precisely to fulfill his call. And everything from his Bible college training to his engineering background to his raising a family—even his time as a New York taxi driver—would be used by the Lord in placing Jean in his native Haiti. An incident that unfolded in 2007 serves to illustrate this point:

It had been a typical day for Pastor Paul. At that time, he did not yet have a vehicle and so traveled most places on foot or by taking a *tap tap*.[33] He had been to the Soge Bank branch he normally used in Marin in order to withdraw $1,200 provided to him by Reformation Hope in order to buy food for the orphans. With the money in his pocket, he walked a good distance down the main street which as usual was crowded with school children, business people, street vendors, and all sorts bunched together here and there waiting on a *tap tap*.

He reached an intersection and left the main street for a residential area along Embassy Street. He located the home of the church deacon and his wife who needed marriage counseling. After a lengthy session, Jean left the modest home and began his trek back to the compound. Not far along the way, Jean was suddenly attacked by three men who beat him severely, stole the orphan food money, and ran off just as suddenly, leaving Jean injured, bruised, and lying in the street.

The most disturbing thing about the assault for Pastor Jean was the revelation that the three men were local Haitian pastors, respected Christian leaders in the community! Eventually the men were arrested and brought before a local court on charges of assault and robbery. As the judge convened the trial, he asked the victim of this violent crime to stand.

---

33 A *tap tap* is a brightly-colored converted pick-up truck, van, bus, or other vehicle used for public transportation in Haiti. The name derives from the sound made by passengers when letting the driver know they have reached their stop.

Jean stood and identified himself to the court. The defendants—the three pastors who had beaten and robbed Jean—were disturbed when the judge looked at them and said, "Do you know that the man you have wronged is an American citizen?"

The magistrate turned back to Jean and said, "Pastor Paul, since you are an American citizen, the laws of Haiti state that you may dictate how these men will be punished. What shall we do with them? You can ask for $15,000 or $20,000, or almost anything you think is just." Jean thought about the interesting turn of events and the judge's question for a moment then replied, "For punishment these three pastors must come to my pastor training classes for the next three months, and they must allow me to preach in their churches." Everyone in the courtroom, from the lawyers to the judge to the defendants was amazed at Jean's reply. The magistrate pronounced the sentence Jean had named and declared the case closed, with a parting warning to the perpetrators that they had better not fail to show up for their classes with Jean. The three men did in fact attend Pastor Paul's classes as the court required. And Jean preached in each of their churches. Today two of these pastors are among Jean's friends in the ministry. Yet he still prays that someday they will all come to see him and restore the children's food money they had taken.

There are echoes in this event in the working-out of Jean's ministry in Haiti of another man of God named Paul, whose own Roman citizenship sometimes proved helpful in kingdom mission. In Acts 22:22–29, Luke recounts one incident in which the Apostle Paul declared his citizenship as he was about to be whipped and interrogated by the Roman authorities. Just as the Paul of the 1st century sometimes disclosed his Roman citizenship and other times found it useful for ministry not to do so, so also Jean Jacob Paul must sometimes reveal that he is an American citizen while at other times he does not.

## Conclusion

In Acts 16:9 – 10, Luke reports that the Apostle Paul received a night vision. And in this vision he beheld a man of Macedonia, *urging him and saying, "Come over to Macedonia and help us."* Paul did not fight the calling revealed so clearly to him in the vision, for Luke adds that, *immediately we sought to go on into Macedonia, concluding that God had called us to preach the gospel to them.*

Perhaps the lesson learned from Pastor Jean Paul is that it is unwise to resist the clear calling of God to go and to preach. Yet few persons are called of God to serve the people of Haiti. And even fewer are chosen and sent in the direct, dramatic way experienced by Jean Jacob Paul. Although it does appear that more recently the Lord is calling more and more Haitians of the diaspora (those who left the country as children or young adults for opportunities in the industrialized nations) to take up the call of Matthew 28: 18 – 20 and evangelize the land of their birth.

Pastor Jean Paul recently celebrated the tenth anniversary of his arrival in Haiti. He continues to pray that God will give him a clear indication — perhaps through the same man from his earlier dreams — as to when he is released from his obligation, as he describes it, to serve the people of his birthplace. This is not because he is ready to leave, but rather because he now labors for Christ in Haiti out of pure joy and blessing, rather than because he has been compelled by the Lord to do so. God has changed his heart and brought him far beyond the perceptions he held on that day at the end of October in 2003 when he first returned to Haiti.

While this work was going through its final composition (May 2013), Jean was again confronted with the realities of serving God's calling in an often unpredictable place like Haiti. In the midst of a custody dispute over a nine-year-old boy named Anderson for whom he had taken responsibility after his parents were killed in the 2010 earthquake, Jean was arrested by the local police and held at the district police station overnight until he could be brought before a magistrate. It seems that Anderson's uncle, who had shown little real concern for the boy, had accused Pastor Paul of violating the terms of his custody agreement. And yet the uncle failed to show up in court two days in a row. Jean agreed to allow the uncle to have primary custody simply in order to avoid the disruption and conflict which seemed otherwise unavoidable. According to Haitian law, Anderson will be able to choose which of these men he would prefer to live with when he reaches the age of twelve years.

A further proof of Jean's distinct calling to share the Gospel in Haiti is his lack of anxiety when things don't go smoothly or when he is facing trial. During the most recent incident involving the local police, Jean spent his time stuck in the district police headquarters sharing the Lord Jesus with the prisoners brought in and out as they went through their processing following arrest. The police officers respect him so much they refused to put him into a regular cell, allowing him to remain in the office area. His congregation members came in droves to pray with and encourage him, and some even brought him a bed to sleep in for the night.

Whether born in Haiti, a past visitor to Haiti, or a child of God who has never even seen the place, Haiti is a rich yet difficult field of kingdom work in which it is essential to test a sense of calling through prayer, through study, through consulting mentors in the faith, and through an on-the-ground experience—a visit in-country. It goes without saying that when a believer enters a field of mission outside of God's call, he runs the distinct risk of proving a stumbling-block to others, rather than a guide to those who need to see Jesus. Just because there are incredibly large ministry opportunities in Haiti, just because there is much spiritual warfare taking place, does not mean that everyone is called of God to go. For some it may also be that the Lord's calling is to support, by prayer and by giving, those to whom the man is waving, urging, saying, "Come over to Haiti and help us."

*This is the home of Pastor Jean Paul's grandparents in La Plaine, Haiti. It is the place where Jean was born and continues to be inhabited by another family.*

*The Souls Winning children supported and nurtured at the orphanage depend upon monthly sponsors who give through Reformation Hope.*

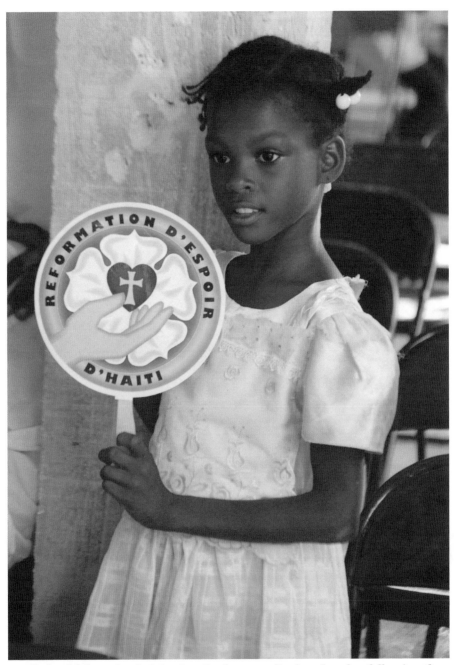

*A little girl from Souls Winning Orphanage displays her fan following the Sunday morning worship. The fan features the logo artwork for the Haitian sister organization to Reformation Hope, Inc.*

*Souls Winning Ministries orphans strike a pose for an Irrigation
Without Borders photo-shoot promoting the benefits of irrigation
for better crop yields.*

*For the Lord your God is God of gods and Lord of lords, the great, the mighty, and the awesome God, who is not partial and takes no bribe. He executes justice for the fatherless and the widow, and loves the sojourner, giving him food and clothing.*

*(Deuteronomy 10:17 – 18)*

# CHAPTER III
## Mission Focus: Caring for the Orphaned Children of Haiti

Jean finally answered God's urgent call to return to Haiti and boarded a scheduled flight for Port-au-Prince. He arrived at Toussant L'Overture airport and was picked up by his cousin. The moment he arrived at his cousin's small home, a strange lady arrived with a string of seven poor children in tow. She said to Jean, "Pastor Paul, I am glad to finally meet you. You see these children with me? You are the only hope they have." Jean replied, "Well, I do not know what you mean. I am no pastor. I am an engineer. And you see I have come here with nothing. I cannot help myself, so how can I ever help these children?"

As Jean watched the happiness drain away from the children's faces, he added, "Well, I cannot help them, but Jesus can do anything for anybody. He can help them." Then he looked at the strange woman and said, "How do I contact you if I can help?" She replied, "That is what I want to know from you. How do I contact you?" And suddenly she turned about face and started running away from Jean and the children as fast as she could. There Jean was, standing in his cousin's small place, looking at seven orphaned children — children who looked to him as their new dad.

Jean was able to persuade his sister to allow him to use a room in her home for that first night with his seven children. After that, he managed to rent a tiny two-room sized shelter just to keep a roof over the orphans' heads until God showed him what to do next. But that wasn't the end of Jean's trouble, for God brought him more and more street children in the days that followed. At one point he was caring for more than twenty children in those two little rooms. Some of them had lost both of their parents in Haitian political violence. Some of them knew one of their parents was alive, but no idea where they were hiding. All of them had been abandoned to the streets, without family nurture, without access to school, and without any certainty they would be able to eat from one day to the next.

Jean Paul's mission, now known as Souls Winning Ministries, began with seven young boys and girls essentially abandoned at his feet. They were street children and orphans, and try as hard as he might, Jean could not get rid of them. He tried ignoring them, walking away from them, and even finally yelling at them. But the orphans simply followed their new father wherever he went like seven small shadows under the bright Haitian sun. Over time, the Lord brought more children to Jean — parentless, starving waifs in need of the Gospel, in need of Christ's love. Soon there were thirty, and by the 2010 earthquake, fifty-six.

Over time, God gave Pastor Paul a clear, bright vision concerning the children multiplying under his care. These children and many others, nurtured as a covenant family, rooted in the Word of God, connected in the love of Christ, and provided a high standard of education will rise up and lead Christ-centered change in Haiti. God prepared Haiti through all its troubled history and now in this time and place, with this emerging generation, Jesus will transform the nation.

With this hope-filled vision for the future of Haiti, Jean resolved that the children cared for at the Souls Winning orphanage would not normally be placed for adoption outside of their native land. By faith Souls Winning sees these children growing up and becoming Haiti's doctors, lawyers, ministers, diplomats, national assembly members, and even presidents. Transformation in Haiti must come from within Haiti, birthed by the Haitians themselves. This new up and coming generation, rooted in Christ, offers just that kind of promise.

There were hundreds of thousands of street children and orphans in Haiti before the January 2010 earthquake. That catastrophic event drove the large numbers even higher. *Prior to the earthquake, as many as 380,000 children were estimated to be living in orphanages within the country. In the post-earthquake devastation, the number of orphans has risen dramatically.*[34] The issue is not whether this is a huge tragedy or even a certain disaster for the future of Haiti. But rather, what is the most effective way to redeem it in Christ Jesus?

Scripture is full of exhortations to care for the fatherless or the orphan. Both terms are used and these exhortations often connect the call to compassion for children in crisis with God's own character of mercy and justice. Deuteronomy 10:18 declares, *He executes justice for the fatherless and the widow, and loves the sojourner, giving him food and clothing.* Likewise, in Deuteronomy 24:19 – 21, concerning times of harvest, dignified provision is expected for the orphan:

> When you reap your harvest in your field and forget a sheaf in the field, you shall not go back to get it. It shall be for the sojourner, the fatherless, and the widow, that the Lord your God may bless you in all the work of your hands. When you beat your olive trees, you shall not go over them again. It shall be for the sojourner, the fatherless, and the widow. When you gather the grapes of your vineyard, you shall not strip it afterward. It shall be for the sojourner, the fatherless, and the widow.

The theme of Yahweh caring for the fatherless also appears in the Psalms. In Psalm 68:5 – 6 David declares that the God of Israel is, *Father of the fatherless and protector of widows is God in his holy habitation. God settles the solitary in a home; he leads out the prisoners to prosperity, but the rebellious dwell in a parched land.* And in the last book of the Psalter, exuberant Psalm 146:9 exclaims of Yahweh, *The Lord watches over the sojourners; he upholds the widow and the fatherless, but the way of the wicked he brings to ruin.*

Care for orphans is most famously preached to the church of the New Testament through the words of James 1:27, *Religion that is pure and undefiled before God, the Father, is this: to visit orphans and widows in their affliction, and to keep oneself unstained from the world.* And James

---

34  Diane Andrews Henningfield, ed., *Perspectives on Modern World History* (Farmington Hills, MI: Greenhaven Press, 2013), 124. Author's note: It should also be taken into account that the figure of 380,000 orphans cited only accounts for those children rescued from the streets or from broken families and listed on orphanage records. The number does not include many thousands more Haitian children of all ages unrecorded and living on the streets.

presents this as part of the outworking of God's compassion through his people — the fruit of genuine, living faith.

The debate at present in Christ's kingdom among those doing work with orphans or street children on the mission field is not a question of "Are we called of God to serve the fatherless?" The question rather is "How are we to serve them?" In other words, what is the most effective and covenantal approach to serving those who are without their fathers and mothers? The question has become rather more complicated during the last few decades. And the catastrophic failures and abuses discovered in some orphanages have caused concerns.

In consultation with Pastor Paul and the Souls Winning Ministries team, Reformation Hope has supported a traditional orphanage facility serving the now sixty-three children since 2007. However, like all missional organizations seeking to be faithful to God's revealed will to provide the best possible care for the fatherless, Ref Hope has gone through an assessment of the four viable directions for future orphan care. These are; continuing the institutional orphanage approach, an adoption approach, a sponsorship approach, and a foster family approach.

Pastor Paul recently received an on-site inspection from a group of officials who assess and license orphanages in Haiti on behalf of the government. Although the government team gave the Souls Winning Ministries facility high marks in meeting the previous official standards (ranked in the top twenty precent throughout the country), they hastened to advise Jean that the Martelly government has recently adopted new orphanage standards promulgated by The Hague in Europe. These new standards include requirements for a program of snacks in addition to the three primary meals, specific space allocations per child, expanded recreational and hygiene spaces, as well as regular dietician consultations. And, as the Haitian government expects to close at least forty percent of currently operating orphanages for being unable to meet these new standards, every licensed facility will be required to maintain a percentage of empty beds/space at all times to receive children transferred to them by the authorities. With these new standards put into place, Reformation Hope and Souls Winning Ministries carefully reevaluated the viability of a traditional orphanage facility.

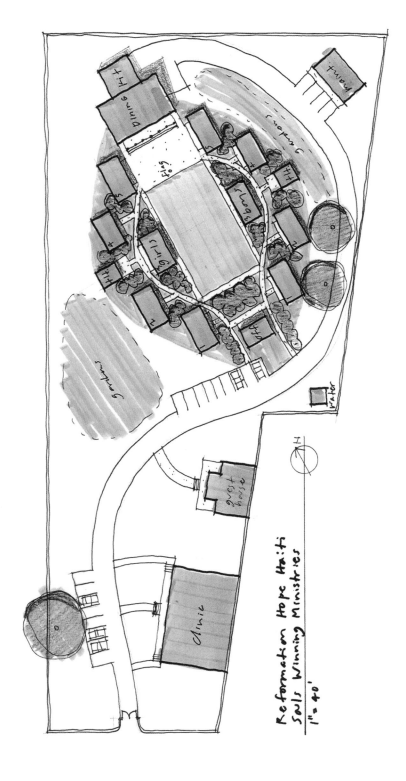

*This conceptual architectural drawing represents one of two designs under consideration for the new Souls Winning orphanage in La Plaine, Haiti. Nebraska architect Perry Poyner is the creative force behind this exciting project.*

## Orphanage Approach

The traditional orphanage model offers some distinct advantages in caring for children who have been orphaned. For example, supervision of the children and management of the various elements of their care is centralized into one location. The children brought into the orphanage environment enjoy the benefits of many 'adopted' brothers and sisters. Some much-needed consistent structure to the children's lives can be created and maintained in terms of hours of sleep, timing of meals, and regular periods of education and recreation. Quite honestly, it is usually easier to raise support for such a system as funding churches, organizations, and even individuals may visit the orphanage and see everything in operation.

It has also been advantageous for RHI to partner with the Souls Winning Orphanage in operating a high quality primary school, offering Bible classes and English training along with the required national curriculum. Providing a good education gives the Souls Winning children an edge for the future of Haiti. Although *education is technically free in Haiti, it remains beyond the means of most Haitians who are unable to afford the supplemental fees, school supplies, and uniforms required.*[35] Souls Winning covers the orphans' primary school uniforms, supplies, and all other expenses. When the children reach secondary school, these are provided for the orphans while they attend a local privately operated high school.

The challenges presented with a traditional orphanage approach are significant. Recent scandals involving child abuse or mismanagement at orphanages in some Third World contexts have underscored some of these challenges. The facility must have committed administrative personnel who understand the importance of the work. Staff members who have contact with the children must be carefully screened and trained well in order to minister to the orphans. The finances of the facility must be carefully stewarded by the management team to prevent waste, fraud, or abuse. Haiti is a context in which organization funds, often provided by overseas donors, are regularly skimmed or applied in

---

35  Timothy DeTellis, *Haiti: Past, Present, and Future — Where Is the Hope?* (Altamonte Springs, FL: Advantage Books, 2010), 73.

more subjective uses than the funders intended. In order to insure the orphans are well-fed, properly clothed, medically cared-for, and solidly-educated, the funds must always be available and well-managed. This requires hard work in relationship building, in accountability structuring, and in outside oversight or on-site auditing of orphanage operations.

## Adoption Approach

Perhaps the most biblical approach to orphan care is direct adoption model, which images in many ways the manner in which God the Father adopted all believers into his covenant family through the work of the Lord Jesus Christ. Adoption offers the orphan inclusion into a more natural family environment and in most cases provides more stablility and relational structure than is possible with the institutional size and requirements of an orphanage facility.

The difficulties in a place like Haiti with the full adoption approach are many. In the first place, few families in Haiti can adequately provide food, clothing, and schooling even for their natural children, making the addition of other children highly impractical. Secondly, while adoption reduces the necessity of much of the staff required by an orphanage, there remains a requirement for monitoring of the adoptive families to insure the orphans are receiving adequate care and provision. Why is this so necessary? Besides the usual reasons for supervision one would have anywhere in the world, *pre-earthquake Haiti had a serious child trafficking problem, with numerous abandoned and homeless children living on the street. It also has a tradition of children living as household servants, many in slave-like conditions, called "restavek," a French word for "one who stays.*[36] Orphans placed in some Haitian homes could be treated as "second-class" members of the family, treated as *restaveks*, or the funds provided for their care might be siphoned off by the father of the household. In Haiti, it is common practice for the male head to spend his income on his own needs to the detriment of the rest of the family.[37]

And the only way this system would be effective in Haiti at the present time is with adequate funding support to these families from outside sources. Shifting from an orphanage facility to adoptive families would save but little money for the overseeing organization, the savings primarily limited to the construction and ongoing maintenance of the physical plant.

Specifically with respect to Jean Paul's ministry to orphans, there is the added complication that virtually all adoptions would be limited to in-country Haitian families. The most viable adoptive approach, and the least expensive for a monitoring organization, would be to allow for the possibility of foreign adoption of Haitian children by pre-screened families. However, this would be in conflict with Pastor Paul's vision. In order to bring lasting, sustainable change to Haiti, Jean believes that it is essential that the orphans under his care remain in Haiti until they are adults. He has experienced firsthand what can happen when children are removed from Haiti and settled in more prosperous countries such as the

---

36  Henningfield, *Perspectives on Modern World History*, 124.

37  Author's note: When stopped on the side of the mountain road between Jacmel and Port-au-Prince I asked Pastor Paul why the only people selling fruit and vegetables along the roads were women. He replied that the women pick the fruit very early in the morning and come to the highway to sell the produce in order to feed their families. If they did not do this, the men of the home would sell the produce and keep the money for themselves.

United States. The truth is that these adopted children seldom return to help their fellow Haitians.

## Sponsorship Approach

Child sponsorships have been a successful model for providing for orphans and street children, as well as impoverished children with a surviving parent, for many decades. Organizations such as Compassion International have created thriving networks with in-country supervision enabling needy children to be sponsored by people from more prosperous nations. And the program unfolds under the auspices of the local church and the teaching of the Gospel. There are many advantages to this system. Large permanent institutional structures are avoided, keeping overhead costs down. The children largely remain in their indigenous culture and relational framework. The integrity of the family (if a parent and/or siblings remain) is preserved and even strengthened. At the same time, sponsoring persons are encouraged to connect with their child, to learn more about the child's culture, and in some cases even to visit their home country. Thus, the sponsorship model offers the promise of two-way ministry. The child receives support and stability while the sponsor is exposed to a world far different from their own. The Gospel has its way in both directions through the linkage created.

The difficulties with the sponsorship model have more to do with economies of scale and with data management which often preclude small organizations or churches from developing this approach. Communication between sponsors and their children is crucial for the covenantal relational benefits to accrue. And the technology aspects of this can be daunting for less well-funded and staffed groups. There are also the very demanding requirements of delivering sponsors' pledge funds in a timely and secure way to the in-country management structure on behalf of the children. Reformation Hope has used a sponsorship model in combination with the orphanage to mixed results. Developing true relationships between children and their sponsors has been the greatest challenge to the program's viability. Changes are being made to strengthen this component of RHI's orphan program. Modern technology enhancements such a mentored, two-way video link will be coming soon.

## Foster Family Approach

The foster family method of caring for the fatherless has much in common with the adoptive approach. However in this case the children are carefully placed with Haitian families who are already members in good standing of the local church — in Reformation Hope's case this would be members of Église Presbytérien in Marin, La Plaine. Under this model, the families would agree to take children into their families while receiving sponsorship support from individuals or churches in the U.S. The funds distributed to these families and the parents care of the children would be monitored by an area case worker (someone hired from the church membership) and also overseen through the diaconal board of Souls Winning Ministries.

## Conclusion

The call of God to care for the fatherless as an extension of his character is unmistakable and unavoidable for the believing individual, church, or mission organization. Reformation Hope shares Pastor Paul's vision of the necessity to care for the orphaned children of Haiti, to share the love of Christ with them, and to prepare them to lead kingdom transformation as the next generation of Haiti's leaders.

The most viable approach to fulfilling this vision is to develop a plan that combines the advantages of the orphanage, the sponsorship, and the foster family approaches. Reformation Hope is now in the visioning stage for the design of a new orphanage facility, sharing space on a new ten-acre compound site which presently houses the recently-built Clinique Médicale de le Réforme (Reformed Medical Clinic).

RHI envisions an orphanage capable of housing ninety orphans plus an additional ten percent empty housing capacity as required by the new Hague standards. The facility would feature separate wings or floors for the boys and the girls — each with separate bathrooms and showers. There will be a common area for meals and a landscaped play area for recesses and recreation. The children will have individual school-style lockers and personal footlockers. And it is hoped that additional available adjoining acreage will be acquired, permitting the construction of both a football (soccer) field and a spacious community center.

The estimated construction costs for this proposed orphanage are presently $500,000, which would be raised through Reformation Hope individual and church investments, and through approaching suitable foundations. The ongoing costs for the facility would be covered through the addition of a sponsorship program for the children in which an interested sponsor will commit seventy dollars per month for a primary school orphan or one hundred and five dollars per month for a secondary school child. Additional cost savings may also be possible through the installation of a full solar power system for the building, for the exterior, and for the ballfields' lighting.

Discussion continues between Reformation Hope and Souls Winning Ministries as to whether additional orphans may be added through a joint foster care and sponsorship program. This would involve employing a model utilized by other Reformed ministries working in Haiti in which street children are placed in foster families connected with the church, and then sponsors from the United States provide monthly support to the families in order to care for the children. As has already been shown, there are so many orphaned children in Haiti in need of the hope of the Gospel, in need of nurturing families, in need of the basic necessities of life, that Reformation Hope and Souls Winning desire to dramatically increase their capacity to care for these abandoned children.

*And they sang a new song, saying, "Worthy are you to take the scroll and to open its seals, for you were slain, and by your blood you ransomed people for God from every tribe and language and people and nation, and you have made them a kingdom and priests to our God, and they shall reign on the earth."*
*(Revelation 5:9 – 10)*

# CHAPTER IV
# Mission Organization: God Calls Reformation Hope Into Being

About three years later, the Lord brought Jean Paul and his children into contact with a certain Mr. Osias, a wealthy Haitian businessman who was not a Christian and who declared his dislike for Jean. Yet Mr. Osias felt that he must help this strange Haitian-American with his entourage of more than thirty children. He decided to sell Jean a small plot of land for eleven thousand dollars and also allow him to borrow the two-storey house located adjacent to the land for six months. "At the end of six months," he told Jean, "if you can buy the house for eighty thousand dollars it is yours. If not, you must move out immediately!" Later on, Mr. Osias dropped his price to forty-five thousand dollars before leaving to receive cancer treatments in Belgium. He also extended his deadline to Jean by three additional months.

Pastor Paul immediately contacted Alan Lutz, Ted Lester, and Martin Hawley, a group of pastors from churches in the Atlanta, Georgia area who had connected with him a few years before in order to provide clothing and shoes for his children. Jean remembered that the same congregations had pulled together to collect clothing, shoes, and other donations for Souls Winning Ministries to raise needed funds through their thrift shop in Haiti. But Jean also knew that this was the biggest thing yet he was asking God to provide and it certainly would be a huge challenge for his American ministry friends.

Immediately the churches in Georgia began meeting and praying to try to discern how to handle this need. Raising eleven thousand dollars for the plot of land had been a true work of God. But could they raise fifty thousand dollars so that Souls Winning could buy that house and legally title it? At first, Hope Presbyterian Church of Marietta, Georgia and Cherokee Presbyterian Church in Canton, Georgia challenged each other and with a matching gift offer succeeded in raising most of the funds needed to purchase the house. God again provided for the children he loves. But it was also in the context of asking God to use them to meet this fifty thousand dollars goal for the orphans, that the Reformation Hope, Inc. non-profit would be born. Reverend Alan Lutz was elected what became Reformation Hope's first president and Reverend James Ted Lester the first vice-president.

While meeting together early in 2007, a few pastors and elders began to realize that Pastor Jean Paul's kingdom work in Haiti was something that they were all called to support — not just on a sporadic basis — but through an organized effort that would promote the ministry more effectively and that would also provide a framework for planning, development, and good stewardship. The group quickly moved from calling themselves a steering committee to hiring a local Atlanta law firm specializing in non-profits in order to establish a 501(c)(3).

Why did this small core of Presbyterian churches decide to create a new mission organization for Haiti? The Presbyterian Church in America already possessed a well-trained and well-staffed sending agency in their own Mission to the World (MTW) organization. The answer was that at that time MTW already had several missionaries and mission partners working in Haiti.

Also, another important consideration was that there were other local churches in northern Georgia assisting Pastor Paul's work that were not Presbyterian in their affiliations. The list included independent Bible churches, an evangelical Anglican church, a Lutheran church, and a Charismatic church. These non-Presbyterian churches were not allowed by their own denominations in some cases to give to another denomination's mission sending agency.

On the other hand, the church leaders who formed what would become Reformation Hope, Inc. were themselves embracing a kingdom vision for Haiti and the Dominican Republic which promoted connecting Christ-professing, evangelical churches and individuals, regardless of denominational labels, in order to proclaim the Gospel throughout the island. They created Reformation Hope as an embodiment of Revelation chapter 5:9 – 10. Christ was busy redeeming for himself *a people for God from every tribe and language and people and nation.* Thus, kingdom mission in Haiti was one aspect of Christ's work in uniting together under the blood of Christ people from every culture, every nation, every economic tier, every race, and every language. Reformation Hope would be an instrument used of the Lord to further the fulfillment of Revelation 5, connecting believers called to mission for the purpose of reaching Haiti and the Dominican Republic with the Gospel.

And as God's Word connects the message of Christ with the ministry of mercy, RHI created a mission statement reflecting that connection which reads:

> The mission of Reformation Hope, Inc. (RHI) is to bring Christ-centered transformation, opportunity, and hope to disadvantaged people all over the world through the application of Reformed Faith principles and material assistance, impacting orphanages and childcare, education, healthcare, food resources, water supply, and micro-enterprise business development.[38]

Reformation Hope's mission outlines the categories of mission and ministry which have driven its work for the past seven years. The statement was deliberately crafted so as to permit the organization to operate in virtually any Third World context. Obviously at the present time the scope of the work is focused upon the island of Hispaniola, beginning in Haiti and expanding into the Dominican Republic.

In conjunction with the specifics of the mission, RHI also drafted a vision statement which sets forth the kingdom principles and kingdom expectations of the non-profit and its partners. The vision of Reformation Hope reads:

> *Wherever the Gospel is planted and takes root, wherever truth and compassion displace ignorance and hatred, wherever future hope is firmly rooted in the here and now, there will be kingdom transformation in individuals, communities, and entire nations.*

---

38 These statements are provided on the Reformation Hope website at: http://www.reformationhope.org/mission.htm and in other printed materials.

*Reformation Hope seeks to serve Christ and serve others as an*
*agent of multinational kingdom hope and opportunity.*[39]

From the outset, it was important for Reformation Hope to understand and embrace where it fit in the Lord's plan to transform Hispaniola with the Gospel. Particularly concerning the nation of Haiti, so much bad publicity and negative imagery had been distributed that calling people to support RHI's work seemed like an uphill task. Eventually the Reformation Hope team realized that God's calling upon them and the organization was not to change the entire nation of Haiti. Jesus was calling RHI to reach out and biblically care for only those Haitians in La Plaine connected with Souls Winning Ministries, the orphanage, the pastors coming for theological training, and any future churches or mission posts which God might establish. The Lord would take RHI's faithful investments in those particular people of God's elect and then use those Haitians to multiply the kingdom transformation of Haiti with the Gospel. The task of Reformation Hope when all is said and done is to obey the Lord Jesus' calling to support Pastor Paul and Souls Winning Ministries in reaching Haitians and Dominicans for eternal salvation and cultural transformation. And it is hoped that Reformation Hope and its partners will create a sustainable and repeatable ministry model for the Haitians and the Dominicans to eventually lead themselves.

---

39  Ibid.,

*One of the most widely-used forms of transportation in Haiti is the bicycle.
It is inexpensive and highly maneuverable.*

*This work, entitled "The Dance," by Pierre Pierre Paul, was painted by the artist in response to his experience of the 2010 earthquake. The painting is from the author's collection.*

*He is wise in heart and mighty in strength*
*—who has hardened himself against him, and succeeded?—*
*he who removes mountains, and they know it not,*
*when he overturns them in his anger,*
*who shakes the earth out of its place,*
*and its pillars tremble*
*(Job 9:4 – 6)*

# CHAPTER V
# Mission Disaster: Earthquake!
# January 12, 2010

Tuesday, January 12, 2010 began as a typical day for Pastor Jean Paul. He left his rented home east of Croix-de-Bouquets and traveled into La Plaine, where the orphanage and ministry offices are located. That morning Jean had a meeting with the orphanage cooking staff. For many weeks now the evening meal for the children had been served very late.[40] This was inconvenient for the smallest children and it was important for the meals to be properly spaced, as in those days the ministry fed the children twice per day. In a rare display of frustration, Jean told the cooking staff in no uncertain terms that if the evening meal was not served to the children on time — about 4:45 p.m. — they would all be fired.

Pastor Paul began his theology class that morning with his regular pastoral students in the new school building[41] and marveled that it was an unusually lovely day. By noon, however, Jean began to feel exhausted, and almost faint. This was a rare thing for Jean, so he decided to end the class early in the afternoon. He sent the student-pastors home, and, stopping by to check on the cooking staff's preparations for the evening meal, gave them a look intended to speed up their preparations. He then

---

40   The main reason for the delay in serving the children's evening meal was the cook staff's reliance upon using charcoal for cooking the food. This is the most common fuel for cooking in Haiti. The Souls Winning Ministries goal is to gradually move to a propane cooking system.

41   The new school building, which was also used for the church's worship services, had been constructed the previous year and dedicated in September 2009.

*Pastor Jean Paul surveys the devastation to the Souls Winning compound following the 2010 earthquake.*

drove back to his home and curled up on his mattress, quickly yielding in sleep to his sudden fatigue.

After some time had passed that afternoon, Jean was awakened by a severe shaking sensation. At first he thought it was a low flying plane, or perhaps someone had hit the side of his house with a car. But as things continued to shake, items fell off shelves, and pieces of plaster and stucco began to fall, he dashed outside. Once the rolling of the earth beneath his feet had stopped, Jean tried to get a visual fix on what had happened. He could barely see ten feet in any direction for all the dust and debris wafting in the wind. Through the haze and smoke he made out the crumbled outlines where neighbors' walls and houses had once stood straight. And then there were the cries for help coming from every direction. He was dazed himself for a few seconds, or perhaps minutes, it was so hard to tell.

Once he came to his senses, Jean's first thought was of his children—the orphans, the staff, his Souls Winning Ministries family at the compound in La Plaine. "Were they alright? Were they alive? What time was it?" he thought to himself. He realized that it must be about five o'clock. "The children must have been in the new school building eating their evening meal when all this happened," he thought to himself. Somehow, someway, he knew he had to get back to La Plaine.

It took some hours for Jean to get to the orphanage. With all of the wreckage, the confusion, and the loss of life, he was stopped many times by traffic jams, roads blocked by debris, and by people in need of help and in need of the Gospel of Jesus Christ. As he arrived on foot at the compound, the anxiousness bottled-up inside over his children, burst out. As soon as he saw the pile of concrete rubble and twisted rebar that once had been the new school—where the orphans typically eat their evening meal—he began running around the compound calling out the names of his children. Some of the orphans would respond when they heard their names. Some came running to their worried father. But it took some time for Jean to calm down enough to hear what God had accomplished.

That afternoon sometime after 4:30 p.m. the children were called in from playing after school to sit and wait for their evening meal. They were inside the new school building expecting to have their dinner when one of the oldest among the boys, *Seker Dorval, yelled at them in Creole, "Get away, dinner is not ready."*[42] Turns out that yet again the kitchen staff was running late. *"Stay outside with the others," Seker told some of the younger children who were cranky and hungry because the dinner was late.*

*Then the earth began to shake and, in seconds, with a crack and a roar and the screams of frightened children, the roof of the building housing the dining room and the church collapsed, pancaked flat down on what would have been more than 60 children and staff members if dinner were on time.*[43]

God in his grace and mercy had spared all of Jean's children and the orphanage staff working at the compound while the earthquake destroyed so much of the Port-au-Prince area and took so many other lives. When interviewed a short time after the devastating quake, Jean commented about how he would deal with his kitchen staff after yet another late meal. He said, *"I will not reprimand anyone. I will not fire anyone. God wanted all of this to happen."*[44]

While Pastor Paul and the children and staff of the Souls Winning Orphanage were grappling with the quake and its aftershocks, millions of other Haitians and foreigners were also affected:

> I was in the restaurant at the Hôtel Karibe with my friend Rodney Saint-Éloi, the publisher at Mémoire d'encrier, who had just come from Montreal. Under the table, two overloaded suitcases filled with his latest titles. I was waiting for my lobster (*langouste*, on the menu) and Saint-Éloi for his fish in sea salt. I was biting into a piece of bread when I hear a terrible explosion. At first I thought it was a machine gun (others will say a train) right behind me. When I saw the cooks dashing out of the kitchen, I thought a boiler had exploded. It lasted less than a minute. We had between eight and ten seconds to make a

---

42  Bob Braun, "Haiti Orphanage Pastor with N.J. Ties Endures with Hope Amid Earthquake Destruction." (*Star-Ledger* on-line edition, January 15, 2010, 1:10 pm), http://blog.nj.com/njv_bob_braun/2010/01/haiti_orphanage_pastor_with_nj.html
43  Ibid.
44  Ibid.

*A young father standing near the earthquake-damaged National Cathedral begs the author for money to buy his daughter some milk.*

decision. Leave the place or stay. Very rare were those who got a good start. Even the quickest wasted three or four precious seconds before they understood what was happening. Thomas Spear, the critic, another of the friends I was with, wasted three precious seconds finishing his beer. We don't all react the same way. And no one knows where death will be waiting. The three of us ended up flat on the ground in the middle of the court-yard, under the trees. The earth started shaking like a sheet of paper whipped by the wind. The low roar of buildings falling to their knees. They didn't explode; they imploded, trapping people inside their bellies. Suddenly we saw a cloud of dust rising into the afternoon sky. As if a professional dynamiter had received the express order to destroy an entire city without blocking the streets so the cranes could pass. [45]

The 2010 earthquake, catastrophic as it was, was not unique in the long history of the people of Haiti. Such quakes had been recorded in 1751 and 1770 in the Port-au-Prince area and there was an especially devastating earthquake on May 7, 1842 which killed an estimated ten thousand people, centered in the north of the country near Cap-Haïtien. However, it is worth noting some factors that made the 2010 event much more destructive. The earlier quakes which struck the Port-au-Prince area in the 18th century were severe in terms of where they would have landed on the Richter Scale, but in that era Port-au-Prince was much more sparsely settled and the people living in structures less likely to collapse or pancake[46], killing their occupants. By the time of the 2010 earthquake, approximately nine hundred thousand people were living in the metropolitan area.[47] Over one million persons on the island were

---

45  Dany Laferrière, *The World Is Moving Around Me*, David Homel, trans. (Vancouver, CA: Arsenal Pulp Press, 2011), 14 – 15.
46  Commercial buildings and private homes in 18th and 19th century Haiti were largely constructed of wood, rather than the concrete, as was the case in recent decades. The older construction techniques are readily studied through the surviving 19th century homes still standing in Jacmel and Cayes-Jacmel.
47  Contrary to some of the officially released figures, Paul Farmer, a note expert on Haiti, gives the population in the greater Port-au-Prince area as 3,000,000 persons. See Paul Farmer, *Haiti After the Earthquake* (New York, NY: PublicAffairs, 2011), 55.

impacted in some way by the quake, including the areas south and east, and northeast of downtown. The death toll, estimated to have been over three hundred thousand persons, was largely attributable to the densely settled and overcrowded housing, constructed of inadequately made concrete block. Port-au-Prince *runs from mountaintops down steep hillsides to the harbor and waterfront slums. It is one of the most densely inhabited parts of the Caribbean and infamous for sloppy, makeshift, and almost entirely unregulated construction.*[48] Structures throughout the city were highly susceptible to the torsion and other motions of the seismic waves generated in the event. These structures had been built more with hurricanes in mind than earthquakes, with insufficient rebar and steel column buttressing. Thus the devastation of lives and property far exceeded anything the people of Haiti had ever seen before.

Another first-hand account from Haitian M. J. Fievre portrays the shock and horror experienced by Haitians on that day:

> A HUGE DUST CLOUD has swallowed Port-au-Prince. The city is in darkness, and lost souls wander the streets. From the backyard, I can hear their voices murmuring then rising into hymns and chants to *Papa Bondye*[49] as they head for safer ground — whatever that may be.
>
> It's just not sinking in.
>
> It can't be Nono sprawled on that beach chair in our backyard, covered with dust and dried blood. My grandmother's legs are stretched out in front of her, and her arms dangle down the sides of the chair. Her chin is slumped down on her chest, her eyes staring down her lap. Her mouth and eyes are open wide, horror crystallized by rigor mortis. *It can't be Nono.* But it is. After the earth heaved and convulsed and our house pancaked on itself, Momma and I used our bare hands to dig Nono out of the debris. Her body was cold when I touched her, and the tracery of red blood vessels in her cheeks drained of color.
>
> The voices of the neighborhood ride and fall in spurts. Momma looks ill and mascara smears across her cheeks. Cupping her face,

---

48  Farmer, *Haiti After the Earthquake*, 55.
49  Creole for "Father God."

I ask, "Are you hurt?" I feel her shoulders and down her arms in search of some injury.

She shivers. "I'm okay," she says. "Freaked out but okay." Her dark face is misted with dusty sweat; a long, powdery black pony-tail trails down her back. She looks confused, bewildered by the newness of her loss.

On Rue Capois, people are still screaming, but the noise is dying as darkness sets. The house next door to ours collapsed too. Our neighbor is dead. Polito was a young dark man with raw, nervous eyes. His voice was thin, like a squeak.

Our other neighbor, Franky, brings us a pitcher of lukewarm water. He says it was a magnitude 7.0 earthquake. "Death is everywhere in Port-au-Prince," he whispers.

I know. I've been outside. I've seen the tiny children piled next to the school, stunned expressions frozen on their faces. The living and the dead here share the same space—the sidewalks, the public plaza, the hospital.[50]

While the earthquake of January 12, 2010 brought unimaginable terror and grief to the people of Haiti in a few brief seconds, and continued anxiety for several days as the tremors persisted, the consequences of the disaster would remain far longer than anyone at that time could have imagined. The earthquake and the resulting popular outpouring of sympathy and support from around the world changed the nature of bringing help to the Haitian people. In God's plans for Reformation Hope this would soon mean a greatly expanded mission and a wider scope of mercy ministry to the surrounding community of the Marin/La Plaine area.

The first three to four months after the quake, RHI assisted Souls Winning Ministries in digging a new deep well at the compound and installing a water treatment system. This potable water became a reliable source of hope, not only for the Souls Winning orphans and the local

---

50 M. J. Fievre, "No Funeral for Nono," in "No Funeral for Nono," in *So Spoke the Earth, Ainsi parla la terre Tè a pale: a Haiti anthology*, M. J. Fievre, ed. (South Florida: Women Writers of Haitian Descent, August 2012), 73.

members of the La Plaine Presbyterian Church, but also for thousands of afflicted Haitians from the surrounding community. By God's grace during the earthquake aftermath, he used the safe water supply at Souls Winning Ministries to stave off the spread of the cholera epidemic into that area.

*Within a couple days of the earthquake, with help from Reformation Hope, Souls Winning Ministries had already drilled a deep well at their compound and began providing safe, abundant water for the orphans and staff, and also to 6,000 Haitians per day from the surrounding neighborhoods.*

*At the same time, the generous gifts from some of Reformation Hope's ministry partners enabled the rebuilding of the wall sections which had collapsed, once again providing protection for the orphans and securing a base for U.S. Marines and other aid agencies to distribute food, water and other supplies in the area.*

*After the June 30, 2013 worship service marking the third anniversary of the rebuilding after the devastating earthquake, Pastor Jean Paul proudly displays his appreciation award from his congregation.*

*For if I preach the gospel, that gives me no ground for boasting.*
*For necessity is laid upon me. Woe to me if I do not preach the gospel!*
*(1 Corinthians 9:16)*

# CHAPTER VI
## Mission Preaching — You Aren't In Kansas Anymore!

Jean Paul introduced one of the American pastors from the Reformation Hope delegation who had arrived to help celebrate the rebuilding of the school and the church after the earthquake. It was a glorious day some six months after the January devastation. The day had begun with a parade about a mile away, a procession of kingdom celebration in fact, which took the same street that the *Vodouisants*[51] used to take in the opposite direction for their dark rituals. With all of the fanfare, the certificates awarded to police officers, scouts, and church officers, and the many prayers and praises, the service had already surpassed some two hours. Even with the relief of ceiling fans and the open windows, the late June heat and humidity of the Haitian plain was rising toward its afternoon peak.

The *blanc* preacher thanked Pastor Jean for inviting him to celebrate such a wonderful occasion in the life of the Souls Winning Ministries church family. And then, at Jean's request, he read from the French version of King Solomon's prayer of dedication for the temple in Jerusalem (1 Kings 8:22 – 61). After a prayer of dedication for the new church to the glory of God in Christ, the American preached a brief message from the text of Joshua 24:14 – 16. It was a short sermon, not only by Haitian standards but also by U.S. standards as well. For there was to be another sermon — the main sermon — preached later by the president of Reformation Hope.

The burden of the Gospel brought by the first pastor was that the Haitian believers must choose between Christ and Voodoo. They could

---

51 *A follower of Haitian Voodoo; term taken from the French "vaudouisant" or Creole used within the English-speaking world.* Felix, *Understanding Haitian Voodoo*, 195.

not have both the blessings of Christ Jesus and the spirits, curses, and charms of the Voodoo system. For too long, too many of them had tried to have it both ways — to blend the light of Christ with the darkness of Voodoo.

A few days after this four-hour celebration of worship and dedication to God had ended, and the Americans had returned home, the first pastor to preach received a call from Haiti. Pastor Jean was excited. He told the *blanc* that a *bokor* had been there for the service and had listened to the short sermon. Afterward the Voodoo witchdoctor professed faith in Christ. Jean reminded the American pastor that God had arranged it all, from his decision to preach the passage in Joshua and challenging syncretism between Christ and Voodoo, to God's compelling the *bokor* to attend the service and then confess faith in Jesus.

The American was overjoyed at such amazing news. And he thanked God for the man's conversion and for the privilege of being an instrument for the Lord's glory. However, the pastor was troubled. He had been traveling to Haiti for several years, preaching at various times and different places, and even challenging the Haitians about their clinging to Voodoo. But, he wondered, was he preaching in a way that most Haitians could follow easily? Was he communicating in a form understood by that culture? And for all his preaching against Voodoo, did he really understand it at all?

Preaching the Gospel in Haiti is different than proclaiming Christ's kingdom in the great American heartland or the Deep South. This has nothing to do with any difference in the biblical Gospel message — but rather with a key difference in the culturally derived communication style specific to each setting. Learning the Creole of Haiti can make a significant difference in preaching more clearly and is essential for those who sense a calling to serve in-country long term. But in discussing the communication 'style', language (even the receptor language) is not what is intended.

The difference in preaching the Gospel to a Haitian audience is especially challenging for those of the Reformed heritage who have been trained to preach, and are accustomed to preaching within a tightly structured, analytical framework. Haitians from an early age are immersed in a narrative forest of stories that serve to communicate the truth, history, and myth that shape their perception of the world. Most Haitians have also grown up listening to preaching rich with stories and illustrations which serve to convey truth and ideas. Much as with the true accounts in the Scriptures, the Haitian is tuned-in to the narrative details, symbols, and action.

The first duty, then, of the American, Canadian, or western European who intends to preach the Gospel in Haiti is to bridge this communication difference which is so fundamental throughout the country. The *blanc* missionary must adjust — not the truth — but the form of communication — in order to reach men, women, and children for Christ. Haitians operate daily in an auditory culture, most lacking regular access to printed materials, or even paper and pen.

The second duty is even more important than the first. Those who answer the call and serve the Haitian people must do more than preach the Gospel themselves — even if they bridge the communication challenges through learning Creole and through preaching narratively. They must also train up Haitians who have a call of God upon their lives to proclaim the Gospel. Is it not better to have a native speaker, converted to faith in Christ and trained in the Word, sharing the Good News with his countrymen than someone coming into the culture from the outside? The answer in most cases is a qualified yes.

It is essential that those Haitian men of God who have an inward and an outward calling confirmed by the church be trained thoroughly in exegesis, hermeneutics, expository preaching, and for some, the biblical languages as well. They must also learn to discern the revelation of Christ in all the Scriptures. But at the same time, care must be taken not to bury the narrative quality of Haitian preaching under the weight of Anglo-American sermonic forms.

What method should be used in order to bring Reformed biblical preaching into the pulpits of Haiti such that it eventually transforms indigenous preaching without destroying its uniquely narrative qualities? This is the question presently under debate among the staff of Reformation Hope. Since its founding in 2007, Reformation Hope has concentrated on providing non-degree track theological training for

CUBA

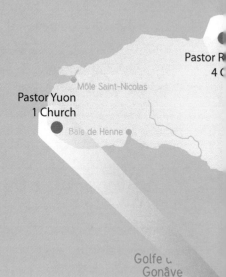

**The Timothy Project**
*This map displays the networks of pastors
and churches involved in receiving
theological training through Souls Winning
Ministries and Reformation Hope, Inc.*

Pastor R
4 C

Môle Saint-Nicolas

Pastor Yuon
1 Church

Baie de Henne

CARIBBEAN SEA

Golfe
Gonâve

Île de la
Gonâve
La Cayenne

Anse-à-C

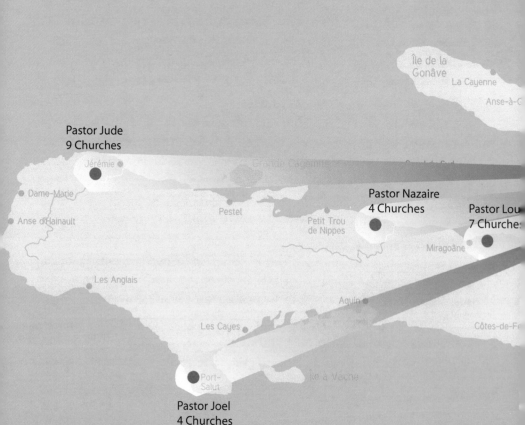

Pastor Jude
9 Churches

Jérémie

Grande Cayemite

Dame-Marie

Anse d'Hainault

Pestel

Petit Trou
de Nippes

Pastor Nazaire
4 Churches

Pastor Lou
7 Churche

Miragoâne

Les Anglais

Aquin

Les Cayes

Côtes-de-Fe

Île à Vache

Port-
Salut

Pastor Joel
4 Churches

CA

# ATLANTIC OCEAN

Le Borgne

Cap-Haïtien

**Pastor Lewis
2 Churches**

Limbè

Fort Liberte

Grande-Rivière-du-Nord

Ennery

Saint-Raphaël

Gonaïves

**Pastor Cherisme´
16 Churches**

## HAITI

**DOMINICAN
REPUBLIC**

Lafond

Hinche

Saint-Marc

**Pastor Cherisme´
16 Churches**

Verrettes

**2 Churches in
Santiago and
Santa Domingo**

Marc

Mirebalais

**Pastor Feurier
3 Churches**

**Church Plant
Batay #4**

**Pastor Fritzner
13 Churches**

**Pastor Paul**

Montneville

Fort-au-Prince

Croix de
Bouquets

**Pastor Cean and
neighboring pastors
19 Churches**

**La Romana
Church Plant**

Pétionville

Léogâne

Port-au-Prince

**Pastor Wosner
2 Churches**

Kenscoff

Goâve

Trouin

Jacmel

Marigot

Belle-Anse

Bainet

**Pastor Charlot
Jacmel Church Plant**

# EAN SEA

pastors using a seminar format. This has been managed through RHI's Timothy Project in an effort to achieve the organization's vision for indigenous kingdom leadership development. American pastors bring outlines prepared on crucial topics for preaching and pastoral development. Haitian pastors and church leaders of every sort, some from large distances, travel to the Souls Winning compound for Friday and Saturday classes. Recently the amount of students and the increasing distances they travel have compelled Jean to begin satellite locations for training in places such as Jacmel, which lies along the southern coast of the country. Those who complete a seminar and pass an exam receive a certificate attesting to their completion of the training. In between weekend seminars, Pastor Paul trains the students on a weekly basis in topics such as the biblical view of the family, biblical church government, sacraments, and The Westminster Confession of Faith.

## Conclusion

Before a U.S. missionary or American pastor attempts to preach the Gospel to the people of Haiti, he should consult resources on preaching using a narrative, or story-telling approach. If his style is heavily oriented toward argumentative development at the expense of illustrations or real-life examples, he should practice sermon development that is outside his normal comfort zone. In most major metropolitan areas of the United States, there are Haitian pastors who would be delighted to assist *blanc* Americans in growing in this style of preaching. And if the missionary or pastor already is partnered with a Haitian who will be his host on the island then this is an ideal context from which help and advice can be sourced. Prior to an evening evangelistic or Lord's Day morning proclamation of the Word in Haiti, have the Haitian partner critique the sermon outline or manuscript and help adapt it to the narrative culture of the congregation.

One other useful point is that a sermon outline, or very brief notes, are recommended for proclaiming the Gospel to the Haitian people. Whereas in the U.S. it is generally preferable to maintain eye contact with your hearers in the service, in Haiti this is very much more so. While the American preacher will typically have a translator working beside him, the basics of good communication still apply to the English-speaking missionary. Frequent eye contact, expressive use of hands or gestures, and modulations of voice are still factors in the Gospel communication transaction, even though the translator is conveying the content. Those pastors and missionaries who have previously partnered with African-American pastors, or who have themselves served in African or Middle Eastern mission fields, will have largely been stylistically prepared for proclaiming Jesus Christ in the nation of Haiti.

Specifically with respect to the vital task of training indigenous preachers and teachers of Christ, some concrete and deliberate steps must be taken in Haiti. The future for Reformation Hope's pastor training, in partnership with Souls Winning Ministries in Haiti, will likely include three components designed to reach a variety of pastors with different educational backgrounds, capabilities, and resources. The three components of pastor training are; pastoral theology seminars, Bachelor of Divinity education, and advanced masters level studies.

## Pastoral Theology Seminars

For some of these current and future pastors, the seminar model, enhanced by periodic in-depth weekday classes remains the more effective means for equipping these ministry leaders for more effective kingdom service. On those occasions in the past when Reformation Hope has offered seminar training, there have typically been several attendees who lacked even a high school diploma, and one or two who were unable to read! There were also some present who were near the age of retirement for whom commencing a multi-year course of regular study would not be practical.

## Bachelor of Divinity Training

The foundational program for those pastor students who possess a high school diploma, certificate, or equivalency will be an on-sight Bible college based in La Plaine at the original compound location. A largely Haitian board has already been established to begin organizing the school and its administration with consultation from Reformation Hope and some other organizations partnering in the effort.

This Bible college, now known as the Académie Théologique de le Réforme, has not yet begun classes. Once the curriculum and program of study are finalized, Haitian students will have the opportunity to enter a program resulting in a Bachelor of Divinity degree. Reformation Hope plans to have the Académie Théologique ready to receive applications for admission in the spring of 2014 with introductory classes beginning in the fall semester of 2014.

## Advanced Masters Level Studies

The highest in-country course of study currently envisioned will allow those students who have successfully completed their Bachelor of Divinity degree to apply for Masters level work through the Académie Théologique leading to the Master of Arts in Religion (M.A.R.) or the Master of Divinity (M.Div.) degrees. Those students deemed lacking in linguistics skills may opt to pursue the M.A.R., which will resemble the M.Div. curriculum without the biblical languages component. In order to further Reformation Hope's vision for indigenous pastor training, those Haitian students who excel and are awarded either the M.A.R. or M.Div. degrees will be offered opportunities to become faculty for the Bachelor of Divinity degree courses.

These highest level students will also be encouraged to pursue Doctor of Ministry (D.Min.) or perhaps even academic doctoral (Ph.D. or Th.D.) work offered through various international or mentored programs. Haitian pastor-scholars who earn their doctoral level degree will be encouraged to begin assuming the teaching responsibilities for the masters level students of the Académie Théologique. The ultimate goal remains that one day, the Académie Théologique de la Réforme will be administered entirely by Haitians and that its entire full-time faculty will also comprised of Haitians and/or Haitian-Americans. American involvement will gradually be reduced to providing specialists and guest lecturers or adjunct professors on an as-needed basis.

Finally, it must be noted that Bachelors or Masters degrees awarded for completion of a theological course of study should have some reputation or standing outside the issuing institution. The Reformation Hope committee tasked with helping the Haitian board of Académie

Théologique de la Réforme believes that while a federal accreditation is not necessary, nevertheless the school must partner with a U.S. — based international school with a reputation for strong academics and recognized degrees. Thus Reformation Hope and the Académie Théologique de la Réforme are exploring cooperative arrangements with organizations such as Miami International Seminary (MINTS), which has a long and sterling track record of fostering theological training in the Third World contexts. The final step in the recognition process for the Académie will be its official registration as a degree-granting college and seminary with the Haitian Ministry of National Education and Professional Training.[52]

*One of the pastoral ministry students studying under Jean Paul makes notes on his seminar outline during a 2013 theology lecture.*

---

52  *Ministère de l'Education Nationale et de la Formation Professionnelle* (MENFP)

*These are some of the VooDoo ceremonial items left behind near the La Plaine farmland, evidence of local villagers employing a bokor to bring bad luck to Souls Winning's Harvest of Hope project.*

*This photo was taken outside a small factory.*

*"Now therefore fear the Lord and serve him in sincerity and in
faithfulness. Put away the gods that your fathers served beyond the
River and in Egypt, and serve the Lord. And if it is evil in your eyes
to serve the Lord, choose this day whom you will serve, whether the
gods your fathers served in the region beyond the River,
or the gods of the Amorites in whose land you dwell.
But as for me and my house, we will serve the Lord."
(Joshua 24:14 – 15)*

# CHAPTER VII
# Mission Challenge: Voodoo and Catholicism In Haiti

A rising clamor was heard from within the walls of the Souls Winning
compound. Jean had no doubt that a crowd was coming down the road
and approaching his main gate. What he couldn't quite figure out was
who they were and why they were coming. After some loud pounding on
the steel gates, Jean let the excited local townspeople into the orphanage.
To his surprise, there were some dignitaries in front of the crowd. Barely
had he admitted them all when he found himself face-to-face with every
bokor[53] and houngan[54] from that side of town!

The chief Voodoo priest from among the delegation approached Jean
Paul and thrust forth his right hand as though Jean should shake it in
return. Just then, a friendly bystander leaned into Jean and whispered
into his ear, "Don't take his hand! If you do you will be cursed and die!"
Jean looked over the confident man standing before him, and after a
brief few seconds, shook his outstretched hand. Everyone was amazed
and horrified at the same time, for all of them were sure that Jean Jacob
Paul was now doomed to the *Papa Loa's*[55] curse.

---

53  *A male Voodoo witchdoctor, who practices black magic or Petro Voodoo.
...the Boker works in secret and charges a fee for his services.* Emmanuel Felix,
*Understanding Haitian Voodoo* (Maitland, FL: Xulon Press, 2009), 191.

54  A male Voodoo priest who practices Rada, *the worship of so-called
peaceful, happy spirits, and has strong links with African traditions.* Felix,
*Understanding Haitian Voodoo*, 194.

55  Literally, *father of spirits*, another name for a Voodoo priest.

The bokor challenged Jean declaring, "It is time for you to leave this place. Get out or die!" Jean replied with determination, "I have news for you. Jesus is taking over in Haiti. This place is not big enough for Christ and Voodoo. You are the ones who must get out! Receive Jesus Christ and leave Voodoo before something bad happens to you."

Jean Paul never suffered for taking the bokor's hand. The Voodoo priest had no power over a child of Christ. The Haitians who saw the events of that day and those who heard about it later were deeply affected. Yet within two years the twelve Voodoo priests working near the Souls Winning Ministries compound were either converted to Christ, dead, or fled to Canada and the United States. People traveling to Souls Winning ministries now pass by eight neglected and derelict temple remains, reminders of the once vibrant Voodoo presence in the neighborhood which was defeated by the sword of Christ.

Besides a working knowledge of its history, anyone traveling to Haiti to spread the Gospel should know some essentials about the Voodoo (or *Vodou, Vudou*) practiced by the vast majority of the people. It has often been stated that Haiti is seventy-five percent Roman Catholic, twenty percent Protestant, and ninety-five percent Voodoo. This may be more popular myth than truly accurate. However, it is quite true to say that the Catholic Church retains the largest share of adherents among Christians and that much more than half of the population practice some form of Voodoo in syncretism with their Roman Catholic worship.[56]

The Haitian fascination with Voodoo derives from the people's ancestral connections with the African continent, which stretch back in time to the arrival of the first slave trader vessels to the shores of Hispaniola. It is deeply rooted in the identities of most Haitian families and over the centuries has adopted many of the trappings and symbols of Catholicism.

Some scholars trace the pervasive influence of Voodoo in Haiti to

---

56 *This religious complex is a syncretic mixture of African and Catholic beliefs, rituals, and religious specialists, and its practitioners (sèvitè) continue to be members of a Catholic parish.* Timothy T. Schwartz, "Haiti." *Countries and Their Cultures*, Carol R. Ember and Melvin Ember, eds. vol. 2 (New York: NY: Macmillan Reference USA 2001), 967 – 978, reprinted in: Diane Andrews Henningfield, ed. *Perspectives on Modern World History* (Farmington Hills, MI: Greenhaven Press, 2013), 133.

a man named Boukman and to an often-cited ceremony in which the Haitian Revolution against the French overlords sought the help of the Voodoo gods or *lwas*.

The popular story of this Bois Caïman[57] ceremony has been embellished by later historical researchers, Voodoo story-tellers, and ordinary Haitians either fascinated or disgusted with the event. In fact, even the date of Bois Caïman has been disputed for many years. What is rarely disputed is that some sort of Voodoo ceremony was performed at the dawn of the August 1791 slave revolt in the north of Haiti.

Part of the confusion concerning the Bois Caïman Voodoo ceremony is that some accounts might lead the reader to conclude that is took place on the same Sunday night (August 14, 1791) as the famous rebellion planning meeting at the Lenormand de Mézy estate.[58] However, the closest contemporary account of the events of the 1791 rebellion in the north clearly indicate that there were two separate meetings seven days apart.[59]

Very few precise details of the ceremony can be verified with certainty. However, as the events of Bois Caïman are so very etched upon the popular consciousness of the Haitian people, a representative account may prove useful. This one is from a work entitled *Histoire du Peuple Haïtien* by Haitian statesman and historian Dantès Bellegarde:

> ... in the midst of a forest called Bois Caïman [Alligator Wood], on the Morne Rouge in the northern plain, the slaves held a large meeting to draw up the final plan for a general revolt. They consisted of about two hundred slave drivers, sent from various plantations in the region. Presiding over the assembly was a black man named Boukman, whose fiery words exalted the conspirators. Before they separated, they held amidst a violent rainstorm an impressive ceremony, so as to solemnize the undertaking they had made. While the storm raged and lightning shot across the

---

57  Bois Caïman is name for the wooded location where this first slave insurrection ceremony is believed to have taken place. Much of the ceremony is obscured in the legends, myths, and the aspirations of the first Haitians to win their freedom.

58  See pages 8 – 9 of this work for details on the rebellion planning meeting of August 14, 1791.

59  For more details on the historiography behind this conclusion, please see, Geggus, *Haitian Revolutionary Studies*, 81 – 92.

sky, a tall black woman appeared suddenly in the center of the gathering. Armed with a long, pointed knife that she waved above her head, she performed a sinister dance singing an African song, which the others, face down against the ground, repeated as a chorus. A black pig was then dragged in front of her and she split it open with the knife. The animal's blood was collected in a wooden bowl and served still foaming to each delegate. At a signal from the priestess, they all threw themselves on their knees and swore blindly to obey the orders of Boukman, who had been proclaimed the supreme chief of the rebellion. He announced as his choice of principal lieutenants Jean-François Papillon, Georges Biassou, and Jeannot Bullet.[60]

Antoine Dalmas, whose work is perhaps the earliest account of the Bois Caïman event, provided additional details with respect to the sacrifice of the pig. He wrote that the black pig that was cut by the priestess' large sword was then offered as *a sacrifice to the all-powerful spirit*. The slaves who drank the blood as part of the Voodoo ritual were surrounded by items which served as magical charms. And some reported that the Bokor Jean-Baptiste Dutty Boukman offered prayer to a god other than the God of the Bible. A translation of the Creole prayer reads:

> God who created the sun, who gives us day, who lifts waves and moves hurricanes, watches over us, hidden in clouds. He sees the actions of the white men. The god of the whites pushes them to commit crimes, but ours only leads toward good deeds. Our god, who is good to us, urges us to seek revenge for the evil done to us. He directs our weapons and he will help us. Banish the symbol of the god of the whites who made us suffer, and listen to the voice of freedom that speaks in each of our hearts.[61]

Whatever the truth may be concerning the specifics of the ceremony, no understanding of the prevalence of Voodoo in Haiti is complete without its mixture of fact and folklore. The Bois Caïman account in modified form was still being taught to the school children of Haiti as late

---

60  Geggus, *Haitian Revolutionary Studies*, 81. Geggus translated Bellegarde's original published account and included it at the beginning of chapter 6 of his work.

61  Emmanuel Felix, *Understanding Haitian Voodoo*, 26.

as 1972 through a textbook entitled, *Manuel d'histoire d'Haïti.*[62]

As was previously noted in this work in the chapter on Haitian history, the official government position regarding Voodoo and Vodouisants softened dramatically during the Duvalier regimes. *Since 1970 the government has acknowledged its practice and has promised immunity to its adherents, a policy that was continued after Papa Doc's death in 1971 by his successor, his son Jean-Claude (Baby Doc) Duvalier (1971 – 86). Hence, since 1972 Vodou ceremonies have been held openly in Haiti, and the age-old persecution by the government, together with suspicion surrounding those who might have denounced local practitioners to religious and government officials have now passed. Oungans and mambos admit their adherence to Vodou openly; and drummers are no longer required to obtain special permits to beat their drums.*[63]

How does Voodoo function as a religion in modern day Haiti? There are many resources that the missionary or minister preparing to serve in Haiti may consult to answer that question. However, as this is such a prevalent component in people's lives and as it involves powerful spiritual warfare, a few basics will now be covered here.

Haitian Voodoo practices are centered around the local temple. There are many of these in every large population area and a good representation even in the countryside. The practice of Voodoo is directed by the local *bokors, houngans,* and *mambos* who have become practicing priests and priestesses of the religion. In most villages and towns the local *houngans* and *bokors* are revered and hold an equal or even superior status to the parish priest or Protestant pastor. *Houngans* are generally classified as practicing 'white' magic, or magic that provides healing or good luck. On the other hand, *bokors* practice the more sinister black arts (*Petro Voodoo*) and spells. *Bokors* typically charge for their services and often become quite wealthy by Haitian standards.

---

62  Alfred Métraux, *Voodoo In Haiti* (New York, NY: Schocken Books, 1972), 42.
63  Leslie G. Desmangles, *The Faces of the Gods: Vodou and Roman Catholicism in Haiti* (Chapel Hill, NC: University of North Carolina Press, 1992), 55. Author note: In connection with Desmangles' statement, I can attest to the unmistakable sounds of the Voodoo drummers at night. This was especially prevalent in the outlying open areas near Port-au-Prince prior to the 2010 earthquake.

Pastor Jean Paul's one remaining unsaved brother, a man named Wilfred, operates one of these Voodoo temples behind his home. He would like to profess faith in Jesus Christ, but does not know how he could ever earn as much money as he presently gets providing curses, spells, and other Voodoo magic to his local clientele. Other customers travel great distances to pay for his services. Wilfred becomes irritated when his brother Jean visits him in his home. It turns out that whenever the pastor arrives, the *lwa* that gives Wilfred his power leaves him and his house, and thus Wilfred cannot earn his living.

The *lwas* are a crucial part of Haitian Voodoo practice and no one from the outside of the culture can fully grasp some Haitian behavior without understanding how the *lwas* work in conjunction with those Haitians who are active *Vodouisants*. Essentially there exists in Voodoo a pantheon of lesser gods or spirits known as *lwas* (or *loas*). An initiate into the religion undergoes a time of preparation and is then brought by the priest into the main courtyard of the temple for the ceremony known as the *Lave Tet*. This Voodoo rite is celebrated to stabilize the *zany* in the head of the Voodoo follower.[64] A *zany* is the Voodoo spirit who has been chosen to "mount" or possess the initiate.

There are male identifying *lwas* and female ones as well. They have very unique 'personalities' and each of them has a Voodoo name. Some of the Voodoo spirits are closely connected with Haitian families. Thus, the children of a parent who serves a specific *lwa* may dedicate their children to the same spirit. Also, depending upon the 'personality' of the *lwa* who possesses the Vodouisant, the person will owe their Voodoo spirit a specific day of dedicated service each week, along with certain gifts and offerings. Sometimes, a male Vodouisant receives a female identified spirit. In those cases, on that spirit's day of dedication each week, the man may not approach his wife for sex, but owes his devotion entirely on that day to his *lwa*. The same is true when a female Vodouisant receives a male identifying *zany*.

Some of the Voodoo *lwas* include Danbhalah Wedo (the supreme god of Voodoo, symbolized by a snake), Aida Wedo (also known as Maîtresse Erzulie, the wife of Danbhalah and identified as a goddess or the Virgin),

---

64  Felix, *Understanding Haitian Voodoo*, 192.

and Erzulie Freda (a consort or wife of Danbhalah and identified as the Queen of Heaven). There are many others and each typically has a counterpart among the recognized saints of the Roman Catholic Church.

The Catholic Church has never officially approved the practice of Voodoo. However, as in many Latin American contexts, Catholicism has been syncretized by the Haitian people with their African spiritualist beliefs. Bertin M. Louis explains that circumstances placed these two religions side-by-side in the lives of the colonial slaves:

> Africans who survived the rigors of the passage from Africa to Saint-Domingue were sold as chattel. Once they reached a plantation, Africans were assigned to slave "tutors" who showed them how to perform different tasks necessary for the production of coffee, indigo, and sugar. *Le Code Noir* prescribed baptism and instruction in the Catholic religion for all enslaved Africans and deemed assemblies of slaves for purposes other than Catholic worship illegal (Simpson 1945). However, elements of African religions and rites were kept alive during secret meetings.[65]

Today one can find Catholic depictions of saints which would be expected to hang inside a parish church or large cathedral instead adorning a niche or wall inside a Voodoo temple. The rites conducted inside the temple include elements one would expect to see only within a Catholic service of worship. The spiritual forces being served, however, have little to do with the Father, Son, and Holy Spirit. Again for the sake of illustration is an eyewitness account of one such ceremony:

> We entered the courtyard of his harem. At the center, there was a temple (a large structure) every bit as big as the Protestant churches in our area. It must have been nine o'clock at night. The ceremony had begun a while before we arrived and the room was packed full. It was filled with followers, each one holding a candle and they were singing songs with enthusiasm. The priest was all dressed in red, in dazzling satin, wearing a miter (liturgical headdress) and a crosier (staff) like a Catholic bishop. The officiating priest was standing majestically on an altar, assisted

---

65 Bertin M. Louis, "Haitian Protestant Views of Vodou," in *Journal of Haitian Studies*, Claudine Michel, ed., vol. 17, no. 1, Spring 2011 ( Santa Barbara, CA: Haitian Studies Association and the Center for Black Studies Research, University of California), 213.

by four altar boys dressed in the same way. He was celebrating a solemn end of year mass. But what particularly drew my attention was that although a natural stutterer, he did not stutter a single time during the ceremony.

At the right of the altar were two empty chairs, reserved for two guests of honor. I sat in the second chair, and my friend who invited me sat in the first... I excused myself and told my friend I had to "go to the bathroom." I went out. And after having relieved myself although I did not think I needed to, I decided not to go back in. Instead, I chose to lean my elbows on a window sill where I could observe everything from afar: my eyes were fixed both on the priest and on my friend. And then, I saw one of the altar boys leave the foot of the altar and go to the "sacristy" from which he came back with a cart, with two bottles of 7 Up and two glasses, each half filled with ice. My friend began to search for me with his eyes. Not finding me, he opened one of the bottles, filled his glass and brought it to his lips. His lips had barely touched the glass when he suddenly put his drink down on the cart, having gone into a deep sleep and was leaning on his crossed arms against the altar.

After the priest pronounced his "Ite misa est" ("Go, it is sent" — mass is over), he went into the sacristy with his entourage. And now, all dressed in white, in bright white satin, they came back toward my friend. When the priest touched him, he stood up with a woman's mannerisms, a temperamental and delicate woman. The officiant dressed him in a white satin robe, and put earrings and a silver ring on him. He was henceforth married, married to a deity, married to Erzulie. The priest preached on how to behave in this world and in the other, in the "Ville Aux Camps."

From that point on, I could say of my friend that he is an *adept*, a *follower*, a *servant*, a *serviteur*, a *chwal*, that he *has his loa* or his *mystère*, that he was *"mounted" by the angels*, or *by the saints*, or *by the spirit*. I could with good reason also speak of his *crise-loa* (loa-crisis), of his Voodoo crisis, of his *possessive state* or of the phenomenon of his *possession* that made him a Voodoo "criseur" or the *temporary temple* of Erzulie.[66]

---

66  Felix, *Understanding Haitian Voodoo*, 67 – 68.

It is obviously important for anyone answering God's call to serve in Haiti to understand the realities of Haitian Voodoo and its oppressive hold upon those who have been "mounted" or possessed by a demonic *lwa*, as well as the indoctrination imbibed by those who attend the temple services. Voodoo is far more than mere superstition and far more dangerous to the souls of its Vodouisants than many Americans realize. In fact Christians in the U.S. should be more concerned than ever with Voodoo and its spiritual forces as more and more houngans, bokors, and mambos are moving to major American cities like Miami, New York, Atlanta, and Chicago in order to set up shop.

Those who have become temporary temples for the Voodoo *lwas* are required to follow a legalistic system of behavior and to provide specific kinds of gifts to curry favor or to satisfy their *lwa*. For example, a Vodouisant possessed by Erzuli is expected to purchase flashy jewelry and fine clothing to appease their mistress. Perhaps one more eye-witness account from ethnologist Alfred Métraux, who made an extensive study of the Voodoo religion, will reinforce the dangers and spiritual oppression endured by its adherents:

> A *loa's* book-keeping is as meticulous as that of a wayside stall-holder. He enters presents received against favors granted, and never forgets promises made. In the course of an invocation of *loa* I heard most revealing remarks in this respect: spirits had been called by Lorgina who wished to consult them about the illness of Tullius, her adopted son. When Ogu-balindjo[67] heard the young man's name he cried out: 'Who? Tullius? I don't know him. Who are you talking about? When told the invocation concerned his protégé, who was ill and praying for help, the *loa* said disdainfully: "That man never gave me anything. Although he earned a lot of money he never gave me a present. He doesn't seem to care much for the *loa*.' Then it was Ezili-batala's turn to complain: "I am root-*loa* of Tullius,' she said, 'he hasn't bought me or even offered me the least little spree. *Sak vid pa kanpe* (an empty sack does not stand up).' With this proverb she let it be understood that the *loa*, offended by the negligence of Tullius, had abandoned

---

67  Ogu-balindjo, or Ogou-Badagri is a male Voodoo *lwa* who had a child named Ursule with the female *loa* Ezili (Ezuli). See Joan Dayan, *Haiti, History, and the Gods* (Berkeley, CA: University of California Press, 1995), 63.

him and refused to come down 'into his head' to protect him from harmful spells.[68]

The connection between Voodoo and Roman Catholicism in Haiti becomes obvious when a more than superficial study of the culture and history is conducted. Many Haitians see little contradiction with attending a Sunday Mass or even a Protestant church service and then spending another night during the week celebrating a Voodoo ritual in the temple down the street. To a very pragmatic and often superstitious Haitian afflicted by poverty, hunger, and disease, it seems the wisest course is to appeal to both realms for supernatural help with struggles in this life. In other cases, the symbols and names of the Voodoo pantheon have been so merged with the Catholic saints and their imagery that it may appear that the two religions are simply variants of the same spirit realm. History certainly has played a significant role in this 'blend' of African spiritism and the established Catholic Church. As Demangles writes:

> The simultaneous practice of Vodou and Roman Catholicism was generated by the historical circumstances in Haiti. As already noted, in the days of slavery, the church found it difficult to convert all blacks to Catholicism. Through intense programs of evangelization, religious acculturation took place and some Catholic concepts took root and appealed to the slaves. But behind the veil of an apparent Catholicism, religious concepts from different regions of Africa became dominant and remained so throughout Haitian history. On the one hand, the maroon republic's isolation from European influence, as well as their residents' struggle in the revolution, engendered the crystallization of African ethnic beliefs and religious practices in Haiti. On the other, the missionaries' efforts to evangelize the slaves resulted in the incorporation of Catholic tradition into the slaves' beliefs and practices. Soon after independence, when Haitian customs and social institutions were being formed, the fifty-six-year breach with Rome altered the nature of Roman Catholicism in the country: Catholic priests who were not concerned with weaning the people away from their folk beliefs permitted Vodou to root itself solidly within Haitian life.[69]

---

68  Alfred Métraux, *Voodoo In Haiti*, 96 – 97.
69  Leslie G. Desmangles, *The Faces of the Gods: Vodou and Roman Catholicism in Haiti*, 55.

One piece of good news from Haiti concerning the warfare between Voodoo and the kingdom of Jesus took place at Cap-Haïtien on May 15, 2005. On that date *Christians numbering approximately 2,000 assembled in the heart of Cap-Haïtien for a three hour meeting of prayer, repentance and worship of the One True God*. At the end of the public time of prayer, which had been led by the town's mayor, the Haitians *invited the kingdom of Christ to descend upon the nation of Haiti, in the name of Jesus. And that all Satanic engagements made in the name of Haiti be nullified in the name of Jesus.*[70]

## Conclusion

The study of Voodoo basics may seem unnecessary to some well-meaning Christians planning to go to Haiti. But the truth is that Voodoo is so prevalent in Haiti that an encounter with one or more of its practitioners is very likely. Those who have developed a working knowledge of this African-derived religion can easily spot its artifacts scattered about the countryside and its images woven into the paintings and metal sculptures displayed along the roadsides. Missionaries who live in-country or who travel to Haiti frequently invariably have stories of direct confrontations, sometimes involving fierce spiritual warfare. One incident involving a Reformation Hope team which occurred in the fall of 2009 provides a sample:

The old bus full of Souls Winning choir members and three preachers from Reformation Hope left the main paved road and began the trek along the muddy ruts leading to the remote village of Campeche at the foot of the mountain.

The group was on its way to Église Presbytérien De Campeche, a village church pastored by Jean Raphael Cean. Although Jean Paul did not share it with his choir or his blanc visitors on the bus, he was pretty sure the group was under spiritual attack. The team arrived for the joint worship service and as they set up for the gathering, Pastor Cean mentioned to Jean that there was to be a Voodoo service nearby about that same time.

---

70  Felix, *Understanding Haitian Voodoo*, 160 – 161.

The church service got going late because the host church's own choir arrived behind schedule — nothing new in a place like Haiti where time is a bit 'relative'. As the typical blend of praises, prayers, greetings, and hymns continued, the light outside began to dim noticeably. Some of the locals from the village who did not attend the worship were visible outside peering into the sanctuary through the decorative steel grates of the widow openings.

Before the Ref Hope minister selected to preach the main sermon ascended the pulpit, Cean warned Jean that things were getting intense and that perhaps Pastor Paul should keep his team overnight there at the church and not venture outside the village into the black Haitian night. Cean even offered to provide some of his church members to guard the team while they slept at the church.

Jean advised Pastor Ganey, the preacher for that evening, to shorten his message substantially because the team needed to leave as soon as possible. After a sermon less than half the usual length, a parting hymn, some words of thanks to the host congregation, and a benediction, the Reformation Hope and Souls Winning team quickly piled into the bus and retraced their path along the winding muddy ruts which served as a road. Once the team was well away from the village and surrounded only by the darkened countryside, the sense of danger was evident for many bouncing along inside the bus.

Pastor Paul could see the signs everywhere even in the inky blackness — at every bend in the road, every crossing, and every place that it was necessary to stop for some reason — the Vodouisants had held a ritual and placed their charms of cursing. It was now absolutely dark as the bus finished its descent from the foothills and into the flat plain — an expanse filled with small farms. The team inside the bus noticed that the driver had slowed way down, slower even than had been necessary in negotiating the giant water-filled craters along the way.

And then it happened — an unsettling and frightening sound, growing louder by the moment, of fists and palms pounding on the sides of the bus. They seemed to come from out of nowhere — from inside the very darkness all around and they were shouting. The primal shouting was in Creole, but the message was unmistakable. Jean translated it as,

"Christians go home! Get out of here! We don't want you here!" No doubt he cleaned up their choices of words somewhat.

The Voodoo procession had met the van after their own dark ceremony there on the plain and sought to overpower the followers of Christ who by now were praying inside. The Vodouisants believed that if they gathered enough followers of Voodoo together that night, if there were enough *lwas* awakened and their powers concentrated against the Christians, they would be able to drive them out and claim victory. By then, one of the Ref Hope pastors was singing the Doxology to himself in praise of God in order to battle against the fear. It seemed effective in refuting the taunts, cursings, and pounding noises created by the crowd. He knew at that moment that he and his brothers and sisters were on the front lines and fighting for the kingdom.

For just a brief moment it seemed possible the Vodouisants and their *lwas* might prevail. The racket created by the crowd outside and the increasing rocking back and forth of the bus made even the strongest begin to wonder if they would ever get out of that dark plain alive. And then, almost as suddenly as it had begun, the noise began to lesson, the pounding seemed to waver, and the driver succeeded in moving the bus forward, past the agitated crowd. By the grace of God the busload of weary kingdom warriors escaped the spiritual ambush and continued then rather quietly the long trip back to the compound in La Plaine. Everyone on the bus that night was thankful to God for victory in Christ. And at the same time, everyone on that bus would never be quite the same again.

The power of Voodoo is no laughing matter. But the power of Christ is unlimited. There is no real contest when Christ confronts the darkness which is Voodoo. But because its presence is real and intense among the people of Haiti, and because it forms such a large part of the background of the culture and of many people's lives, the servants of Christ must understand its basics and prepare to face it and its followers only in the power of the Spirit of Christ.

Reformation Hope strongly encourages its first-time short-term mission team members to read material to acquaint them with the general practices of Haitian Voodoo and especially its real and its imagined effects upon its Vodouisants. One very helpful resource, which does not require an extensive amount of time to read, is *Understanding Haitian Voodoo*, authored by Emmanuel Felix, Jr. It is unfortunate that a great many missionaries and ministers traveling to Haiti have either ignored the very real forces at work in Voodoo, or have called its Vodouisants to abandon it for Christ's sake, while never truly understanding it themselves. A basic comprehension of Haitian Voodoo is essential — just as comprehending its history — in order to properly understand and relate to the people of Haiti and apply the Gospel effectively as Christ's called and appointed physicians of souls. Just recently Reformation Hope staff encountered the remnants of a Voodoo ritual carried out near the Harvest of Hope farming project in La Plaine — probably conducted in order to put a curse on the initiative.

Proclaiming the kingdom and its transforming power is always intense spiritual warfare. Preaching the Gospel in Haiti means delivering souls from bondage to the demons of Voodoo and guiding them to freedom in Christ. This battle for the eternal destiny of souls unfolds along the frontlines every day in Haiti's cities, churches, medical clinics, tent camps, and village shacks. Therefore anyone planning to enter the Haitian mission field must have the covering power of prayer in their work. Besides their own prayer life, it is essential for the missionary or pastor to have a prayer team at work on their behalf daily, before, during, and after their trip. While the forces of evil veiled inside the ceremonies and trappings of Voodoo are certainly real, they cannot defeat the servants of Christ and the weapons of his servants — the Word and prayer.

*Souls Winning Ministries and the Presbyterian Church of La Plaine march in joyful procession from the new medical clinic building site to the original church and orphanage. The parade moves along the same street once used by the local Haitian Voodoo priests.*

*The staff of Souls Winning Ministries and the Jean Raphael Cean's construction crew work feverishly the final days in June leading to the new church's dedication.*

*On June 27, 2010 the congregation of the Presbyterian Church in La Plaine concludes their parade at the entrance to their new church. A service of celebration and dedication was held inside the new sanctuary.*

*And we know that for those who love God all things
work together for good, for those who are called
according to his purpose. For those whom he foreknew
he also predestined to be conformed to the image of
his Son, in order that he might be the firstborn among
many brothers. And those whom he predestined he
also called, and those whom he called he also justified,
and those whom he justified he also glorified.*
*(Romans 8:28 – 30)*

# CHAPTER VIII
## Mission Reprise: Rebuilding Hope In Haiti

A short time after the earthquake of January 12, 2010, a small team of
Reformation Hope staff arrived by plane in Santo Domingo, the capitol
of the Dominican Republic. In those early days of search and relief, it was
virtually impossible for non-government, non-military, or non-medical
people to fly into Port-au-Prince directly. In fact, there were huge air
traffic and logistical management problems at Toussaint Louverture
International Airport for weeks following the earthquake.

The Reformation Hope team was picked up by Jean Paul and after
spending the night in Santo Domingo, began the long seven to eight hour
trek to the ministry compound in La Plaine, Haiti. The trip along the
roadways of the Dominican frontier was uneventful, with the exception
of a flat tire. During the crisis, the usually tight border crossing between
these two nations was no where to be seen and the team simply crossed
the two checkpoints without interruption as part of an impromptu motor-
cade of United Nations, UNICEF, Red Cross, and other organizations'
cars, vans, and trucks.

No one on that team noticed anything unusual on the Haitian side
of the border at first. The only indication of the disaster were the huge
numbers of relief vehicles clogging the main road. However, the closer
the Reformation Hope team got to the Croix-de-Bouquets and Marin
area, the more the signs of a severe earthquake increased. Jean pointed
out to the team members some disturbing reminders of the quake along

their path. "There!" he would say, "That used to be a three-storey school which collapsed in the quake. Many children and teachers are still buried inside." "And look there," he would quickly point out the other window, "That church was destroyed. Thank God no one was inside." The team couldn't help but notice while driving past a large cemetery, that some of the graves and the tombs had broken open. Coffins were visible in several places. Markers lay strewn all about.

The Reformation Hope assessment team arrived at the compound in La Plaine and were greeted by virtually the same sight Jean had seen days before. All that remained of the beautiful new school building, dedicated the previous September, was a flattened pile of layers of shattered concrete and twisted rebar. Everyone gazed at the leveled building for some time. Jean picked-up a huge chunk of the concrete rubble. Everyone was thinking the same thing. But for the grace of God some fifty-seven children and a few staff would have been inside that building when the earthquake struck. And then it dawned on them in an intense way. God had delivered those children and those staff members for a purpose and for his good plan.

The next morning was the Lord's Day and so the Reformation Hope staff returned to the compound to worship with the Haitian brothers and sisters and also began planning the way forward. What a scene greeted the RHI team as they entered the gates! The orphans were standing with Pastor Jean, all dressed in their Sunday best, upon the ruins of their school. Jean delivered a video interview from atop that rubble for all the ministry partners of RHI. Even as he was standing upon the ruins of a once bright dream, he shared that God was able to rebuild its promise, much, much more gloriously than what had stood there before. He declared by faith that, "God had spared his children, not because we are so good, but because God is so very great!"

Although the building used for worship had been destroyed, the brothers and sisters had rented a tent and arranged some chairs and God was glorified in the praises of his people while promises were made that hope would again be established with Souls Winning Ministries. Letters of support and encouragement from brothers and sisters in the United States were read to the congregation. The children — all survivors by

God's amazing grace — sang hymns of praise to Christ their Savior. And before the team began the long trip back to Santo Domingo, a solemn pledge was made according to faith, that God would restore all that had been taken away, a promise that what was coming would be even more amazing than that which had stood there before.

The weeks immediately following the earthquake were anxious ones for the U.S. staff of Reformation Hope. While the children were dramatically saved by God through the late supper, two hundred and thirty-eight members of the Souls Winning church in Marin, Eglise Presbyterien D'Haiti, lost their lives — one fifth of the total congregation in January 2010. Pastor Paul began the overwhelming work of burying the dead and comforting the grieving families of his church and his community. And the on-site Reformation Hope visit shortly after the quake left the organization with a huge list of questions about how to go forward. The most essential among them were:

1.  Should the school be rebuilt, and of so, how would God provide the necessary funding?
2.  How would God have Reformation Hope minister to the devastated community through Souls Winning Ministries?
3.  What kind of contingency plan should Reformation Hope put in place for leadership continuity in Haiti, a country susceptible to severe hurricanes, violent political upheavals, and now apparently strong earthquakes?

The utter destruction of the recently dedicated school, which also served a dual purpose as the Église Presbytérien D'Haiti place of worship, was a tremendous blow to the ministry's operations. Within a few seconds the earthquake had shut down the David Petro Christian Academy, crowded the orphans back into the original two-storey house, and returned the church's worship gatherings to the open air.

It quickly became apparent that the Lord would be pleased to have the school rebuilt just as Jean declared during the Reformation Hope post-earthquake visit, "even better than before." What precisely was needed in terms of a new facility? As is always the case in a reconstruction effort, the great challenge was funding the project.

Reformation Hope knew what was needed at the compound through meetings with Pastor Paul and the Souls Winning staff. They also knew the ministry in La Plaine was growing — not despite the earthquake but rather as a result of it. And so the plan called for an improved school, built to the new earthquake resistance standards, as well as an additional building — a separate facility for the worship of the Église Presbytérien.

The estimated price tag for this "even better than before" vision for Souls Winning Ministries came to $300,000. The question still remained. How was this all to be funded? Obviously it was important for the Haitian church members to contribute to this new effort. Yet the congregation lacked the financial means to carry this great load. And so a challenge again went out to the regular partners of Reformation Hope in the United States: "Help rebuild hope in Haiti." It seemed an impossible task at the time. But God, who owns all the cattle on all the hills, already had prepared the resources that were needed. He orchestrated one of many kingdom partnerships to achieve his plan.

Approximately three years before the 2010 earthquake, two pastors, Alan Lutz and Martin Hawley, who later helped organize Reformation Hope, approached the Presbyterian Church in America's (PCA) sending organization, Mission to the World (MTW) in order to introduce them to Pastor Jean Paul and Souls Winning Ministries. The goal was to have Jean become a partner with MTW. At that time, however, MTW already had three mission partners working in Haiti and faced limited resources for the country. It was simply not yet God's timing for Pastor Paul.

But in the aftermath of the earthquake an MTW disaster response team was dispatched to Haiti. Three years after Jean's visit to MTW there were less Haitian partners working with Mission to the World and there was also a growing outpouring of PCA churches compassionately and generously giving to address the disaster. The Mission to the World staff rediscovered Reformation Hope materials in their offices from the prior discussions and determined to visit the Souls Winning compound in Marin/La Plaine as part of their response assessment.

Upon their arrival on Good Friday, March 2010, the MTW team observed something they hadn't seen anywhere else on that trip. Instead of heaps of rubble and despair, the team met an optimistic Jean Jacob

Paul and observed that a new well had already been dug with a water treatment system attached. The water from the well was being provided to locals from the community to help prevent the spread of disease and dehydration. And the old compound wall, which had suffered severe damage in the quake, had been rebuilt. The team also observed that the pancaked school building was cleared away and that a new foundation was being laid.

After a careful assessment, Mission to the World contacted Reformation Hope and a partnership to rebuild the school and to add a church was forged. As the regular Reformation Hope partners and churches raised more than $150,000 for the rebuilding effort, MTW provided the other half of the funds needed from the outpouring of generous giving of PCA churches in response to the January disaster.

By the last weekend in June of 2010, both the school and the church were completed and a celebration of dedication took place. The dedication day began with a parade — not just any parade — but a kingdom-proclaiming, hope-returning parade. As if to symbolize the victory of Christ over Voodoo and the triumph of the kingdom over the earthquake, the procession of choirs, boy and girl scouts, pastors, church officers, and members, with a full marching band in the lead, traveled the same road to the compound once used by the Vodouisants for their sacrificial rites. There were two key differences. First, the celebrants of Gospel hope in this 2010 parade were proclaiming Jesus as King of Haiti, not the Voodoo *lwas*. And second, the parade traveled the opposite direction from the soccer field to the new church at the Souls Winning compound, inverting the processional practice of the Vodouisants.

The believers from the parade were joined by many others waiting at the entrance to the new church building. Together, they processed into the sanctuary while the band continued playing a Haitian variation of "When the Saints Go Marching In" from the courtyard in front of the church.

The three to four hours of worship were a vibrant celebration of the transforming work of Christ and the restoration of real hope to the people of Souls Winning Ministries and the believing community of Marin/La Plaine. And the rejoicing continued as a full meal was shared together by some two thousand people in attendance. For many, this was their only full meal through the entire week. Some of them had not seen such a lavish meal since before the earthquake some six months before. How appropriate the fellowship meal celebration was as a continuation of thanksgiving to God and a foretaste of the Wedding Supper of the Lamb!

The story of the rapid rebuilding of the David Petro Academy and the construction of Église Presbytérien D'Haiti within six months from the destruction of the 2010 earthquake was, sadly, a rare example of progress during the first few months in rebuilding hope among the people of Haiti. And the community celebration of the successful rebuilding of the La Plaine facility near the six-month anniversary did not represent the general disappointment at the pace of reconstruction throughout most of the rest of Haiti. As Chris Herlinger reported at that time:

> Six months later, it was disheartening to see how little had changed. It was true that Parts of Port-au-Prince looked marginally better, as at least some debris had been removed. But generally, the capital city looked beaten down and felt as if it were at a standstill. In some ways a pause was actually needed. Few Haitians I spoke with on July 12, 2010 dwelled on the six-month anniversary of the quake. It was an artificial marker for U.S. journalists and aid workers, who were connected to the outside global media cycle. Haitians were looking only for a break from hardship, misery, and blight. Instead of the anniversary, they focused on the welcome distraction of the World Cup—many people believed that if it were not for the World Cup, the streets of Port-au-Prince would have been filled with protestors, exasperated by the Haitian government's inaction. "People are waiting for someone to show the way to the right place," one of the young Haitian humanitarian workers with the Lutheran World Federation said about the need for leadership and inspiration.

> People I spoke to freely acknowledged that the continuing work of repairing, rebuilding, and rehabilitating Haiti had been hindered by endless obstacles and enormous challenges. Haitian aid worker Sheyla Marie Durandisse said, "If you look at the numbers of those we have served, it is impressive. But compared to the continued needs, you see challenge after challenge." Durandisse's

colleague, Jean Denis Hilaire, was even more stark in his assessment. "It is like a drop of water in the bucket. There is so much to do."[71]

While God had permitted Reformation Hope and Souls Winning Ministries to partner with other organizations in achieving a remarkably rapid recovery of facilities and ministry services, little had changed for the majority of Haitians dislocated by the great earthquake six months before. And as the months continued rolling by since the disaster, reaching to more than a year later, according to investigative reports, the situation had improved very little:

> One obvious change to Haiti's social landscape specifically brought about by the earthquake serves as its most powerful symbol, a constant reminder of the continued impotence of the Haitian state and failures of international aid. Called "tent cities" or "camps," the city of Port-au-Prince now bears on full public display scars of the extended misery. At the peak in the summer of 2010 the International Organization for Migration (IOM) registered 1.3 million IDPs living in 1,300 camps, with over 800 within the greater Port-au-Prince area. As of May 2011, there were still more than 600,000 people living in the camps, according to IOM estimates.

> One shudders to think of this new reality becoming a permanent fixture in Haiti's urban landscape. At their best, camps are planned relocation sites with temporary shelters. "T-shelters," made of treated plywood and social services such as security patrols, water, maintained toilets, clinics, and some simulation of a school. This describes barely a handful, as the contracts for services such as water and sanitation began to run out the first part of 2011. What remains of the clinics are empty and ripped tents emblazoned with fading NGO or UN agency logos. Unfortunately the residents themselves also remain. According to research conducted by Mark Schuller in the summer of 2011, 90 % of camp dwellers were renters before the earthquake. In addition to the slow pace of rubble removal and house repair or construction wherein the vast majority of the more than 175,000

---

71 Chris Herlinger and Paul Jeffrey, *Rubble Nation: Haiti's Pain, Haiti's Promise* (New York, NY: Seabury Books, 2011), 4 – 5.

housing units in need of repair or demolition still await action, a disaster capitalism on an individual level combined with the invasion of NGOs in need of housing has driven rental prices for safe housing through the roof.[72]

Despite the huge amounts of relief and rebuilding money raised in the quake's aftermath, despite the pledges of governments, NGOs, and the United Nations, little had been accomplished more than 12 months after the earthquake of January 2010. And as of the writing of this work more than three years since the disaster, the situation of the ground in Haiti has not substantially changed for those trapped in the sprawling tent cities. Some of the challenges slowing down the recovery effort include; the reluctance of NGOs to release millions of dollars in funds, a lack of infrastructure for managing and delivering recovery services, and insufficient Haitian government resources and mechanisms.

Earthquake-ravaged homes, schools, businesses, and churches are still visible in the Port-au-Prince metropolitan area. Hundreds of thousands of Haitians forced into the tent cities when their homes were destroyed remain in the squalid camps with names like Canaan 1 or Canaan 2. Foreign aid seems stuck in the relief phase when what is needed is recovery, permanent housing, and development assistance. And the Martelly government appears ineffective in leading the Haitian people forward from the rubble into a brighter, greener future. It will take far more than a "Haiti Is Open for Business" public relations campaign to bring about a reborn Haiti. It will take the Gospel and it will take vast resources applied in new ways.

## Conclusion

Where is Haiti's hope being restored and who is God using to rebuild it? While the conditions throughout the country remain bleak and discouraging to the casual observer or aid worker, the missionaries and ministers who continue to answer the call to serve in Haiti see instead a nation whom God has prepared to receive the certain hope of the Gospel of

---

72 Mark Schuller and Pablo Morales, *Tectonic Shifts: Haiti Since the Earthquake* (Sterling, VA: Kumarian Press, 2012),111 – 112.

Jesus Christ. Reformation Hope is committed to continuing the recovery of hope in Haiti through advancing the Gospel, ministering in mercy to immediate physical needs, and equipping the people of Haiti to sustain themselves in the future.

In partnership with other like-minded missionaries, ministers, and missional organizations, RHI envisions the Lord *working all things together for good, for those Haitians called according to his purpose.* Reformation Hope deems it to be the will of God to transform Haiti with the Gospel, while rebuilding its hope in a very tangible and observable way. As the Prophet Isaiah wrote of the Lord's restorative promise to his people, so RHI sees the mercy and power of God applied to the lingering devastation of Haiti and its people, redeemed in the blood of Christ:

> to proclaim the year of the Lord's favor,
>   and the day of vengeance of our God;
>   to comfort all who mourn;
> to grant to those who mourn in Zion—
>   to give them a beautiful headdress instead of ashes,
> the oil of gladness instead of mourning,
>   the garment of praise instead of a faint spirit;
> that they may be called oaks of righteousness,
>   the planting of the Lord, that he may be glorified.
> They shall build up the ancient ruins;
>   they shall raise up the former devastations;
> they shall repair the ruined cities,
>   the devastations of many generations.
> (Isaiah 61:2-4)

*The selling of produce is one of the most frequent and most reliable categories of small business in Haiti.*

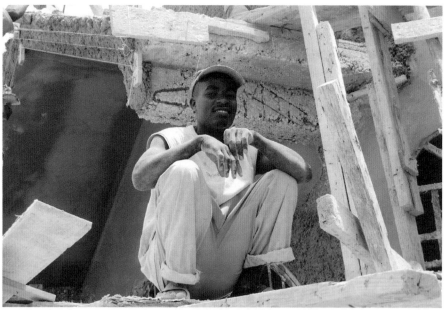

*Since the disastrous 2010 earthquake, the building trades have proved to be good sources of steady income for skilled Haitian carpenters and masons.*

*"When the Son of Man comes in his glory, and all the angels with him, then he will sit on his glorious throne. Before him will be gathered all the nations, and he will separate people one from another as a shepherd separates the sheep from the goats. And he will place the sheep on his right, but the goats on the left. Then the King will say to those on his right, 'Come, you who are blessed by my Father, inherit the kingdom prepared for you from the foundation of the world. For I was hungry and you gave me food, I was thirsty and you gave me drink, I was a stranger and you welcomed me, I was naked and you clothed me, I was sick and you visited me, I was in prison and you came to me.' Then the righteous will answer him, saying, 'Lord, when did we see you hungry and feed you, or thirsty and give you drink? And when did we see you a stranger and welcome you, or naked and clothe you? And when did we see you sick or in prison and visit you?' And the King will answer them, 'Truly, I say to you, as you did it to one of the least of these my brothers, you did it to me.'*
*(Matthew 25:31 – 40)*

# CHAPTER IX
## Mission Shifts: Establishing Sustainable Mission Methods

Haitian Dieuny Peterson Brun had a big idea. He observed that beside a main intersection in La Plaine, called Lathan, every day thousands of people passed by — some of them walking to work or the market, some of them waiting on a *tap tap*, some of them to hire a motorbike to take them somewhere. And he thought to himself, what a great location for a cold drink stand!

Peterson brought his small business concept to the Souls Winning Ministries micro-finance team, who were partnering with Reformation Hope and Pacific Crossroads Church (PCC) of Santa Monica, California. After a careful planning and assessment process conducted by Zafèn, a

Fonkoze partner organization[73], Reformation Hope and PCC provided a one thousand eight hundred and fifty dollar microfinance loan to Peterson.

With the initial loan, Peterson began Kay Zouk-Zouk, a sidewalk beverage stand. He also wisely connected with another enterprising Haitian who was operating a successful food stand nearby. Peterson was not planning to sell food and the woman working nearby had no plans to sell drinks. It was a natural combination for cross-selling between the two businesses. Using good stewardship, careful budgeting, wise reinvestment, and his own natural, engaging marketing personality, Peterson successfully repaid his initial loan on time.

In a very short time, Peterson approached Reformation Hope and Zafèn with a vision to expand Kay Zouk-Zouk by adding a portable generator, a freezer, and three additional tables with chairs to handle the increased customer traffic. Mr. Brun was approved for a second microfinance loan of one thousand eight hundred and fifty dollars, expanded his drink business, and again entirely repaid his loan. Peterson now has another business development idea. He has hired his brother to manage Kay Zouk-Zouk while he converts his pick-up truck into a new *tap tap* passenger service. Peterson truly represents the entrepreneurial hope of a new Haiti reborn from the inside.

The true story of Peterson Brun is the story of a reimagined Haiti. It is the promise of real opportunity which can break the cycle of co-dependency between the Haitian people and the prosperous nations who keep it going through measured hand-outs, often with tangling strings attached. The way forward is through sustainable growth and development with profitable returns, run according to ethical practices, visioned, planned, implemented, and operated by the Haitians themselves.

For too long Haiti has been used as a cheap labor resource and as a

---

73 *Zafèn is a funding source for growing Haitian businesses and social projects that do not qualify for traditional bank loans and otherwise would not have access to capital. Fonkoze Financial Services (FFS) is a Haitian commercial microfinance institution that takes profitable branches and well-tested products from Fonkoze and expands them, reaching hundreds of thousands of Haitians, especially those living in the hardest-to-reach rural areas. For more details see:* https://www.zafen.org/en/about/about *and* https://www.zafen.org/en/about/partners#fonkoze.

charity case by the United States, Canada, and France. During the past two centuries, businesses were largely owned by wealthy foreigners or by the Haitian elite, comprising five percent of the population. The profit earned from these businesses due to cheap labor often fled the country, depriving the nation of much-needed capital while providing no opportunities for common laborers to rise above the poverty level. Further, when large employers — for example the Haitian-American Sugar Cane Company — pull out of Haiti, the economic consequences in unemployment and lost wages are immense.

On the other hand, while a colonialist sort of capitalism has significantly ravaged the nation, all of the NGO relief and aid handouts have created no incentive for Haitian achievement or ingenuity. Instead, a virtually unbreakable bond of co-dependency has been created. The sustainable economic solution must lie somewhere else. And Reformation Hope believes that smaller missional organizations, churches, and even entrepreneurial individuals may be used of God to assist Haiti from co-dependence on foreign aid or from large institutional investors with foreign priorities into sustainable economic growth and independence.

The most effective means to bring about this end is that experienced by Peterson Brun. Through a modest capital investment, which is fully repaid as a loan, an entrepreneur like Peterson can create a small business which generates a living income from which a family can be supported and sustained. Once the loan is repaid, the funds become available for another small business visionary, or even for the expansion of the original business. Perhaps in time a micro-enterprise like Peterson's may grow enough to employ additional Haitians, who then in turn can support their families and begin to build a better life.

## Conclusion

Clearly foreign economic involvement in Haiti in the past has done more harm than good to the nation and its people. On the one hand, heavy-handed large business practices by foreign national corporations have stripped the land of resources while giving little to its underpaid workforce in exchange. On the other hand, in many case with the very best of intentions, foreign aid and relief agencies have dispensed untold millions of dollars and more than that in food and materials which has created perhaps the most dependent nation-state in the modern era. A co-dependency of sorts now exists between the hand-out nations of the U.S., France, and Canada, and the desperately poor nation of Haiti.

In order to address this unsustainable and intolerable situation for the people of Haiti, Reformation Hope seeks to bring training in biblical business practices, mentoring in business start-ups and development, and seed money for planting a crop of micro-finance small enterprises that have the potential to change the country, empowering it to be again a prosperous, vibrant nation. Haiti will one day again be known as the Pearl of the Caribbean.

What sorts of businesses will Reformation Hope nurture and assist to grow in Haiti? Peterson's start-up meets a need in the market in Haiti. His business is an example of opportunities which exist in the food service sector. Joseph Osseille, an administrative assistant to Pastor Paul, has recently also taken out a micro-finance loan through Zafèn. His business, a pasta restaurant, employs two other Haitians.

RHI also sees great potential in Haitian coffee. One of the pastors Jean Paul trains on a regular basis, named Samuel, purchases raw coffee beans from partners with farms in the Haitian mountains. He then brings the beans into La Plaine, roasts and grinds them himself, then packages the coffee for distribution in Haiti at a competitive price. Reformation Hope promotes the sale of his coffee product to Americans visiting in Haiti, who then buy the product and share it with friends in the United States. Samuel's coffee would make an excellent candidate for exportation for sale in the U.S. Haitian coffee used to supply the majority of the European market two hundred to three hundred years ago. And Haitian coffee has been successfully re-introduced into the U.S. market through organizations such a Singing Rooster.

Haitian art is truly unique, energetic, and colorful. Reformation Hope plans to support the work of young Haitian artists — those who are believers in Christ and work without Voodoo symbolism — through micro-financing and consulting help from American artists as to marketing and exhibition techniques. And as with coffee there are expanding opportunities for retailing Haitian art and textiles in the United States and elsewhere in the developed world.

Micro-financing for small businesses embraces other primarily local Haitian sectors. Reformation Hope currently provides business skills training to a group of Haitian men and women who have visions for businesses catering to their own people. Current proposed business projects include: sewing shops, computer repair, bakeries, automobile repair, bicycle repair, and a modest clothing shop. These cottage and sidewalk industries, if run properly, can be extremely profitable in Haiti. The keys to success are their small scale, quality service, and their ability to meet a felt need in the local community.

RHI also supports the development of a farming business operated by a team of ten men connected with Souls Winning Ministries. The farm is designed to operate in a sustainable way and will soon feature a S.M.A.R.T. water technology irrigation system. The project provides not only employment and training in agriculture (through a Master Farmer certification program), but also generates income for the Haitian mission through the sale of cash crops such as plantains and cassava. In addition, Souls Winning has embarked upon developing a goat farm, which promises both income for the ministry and additional protein for the children in the orphanage.

Whether a big non-governmental organization (NGO) or a Christian missional organization, the most sustainable economic assistance that can be provided to the Haitian people is some form of micro-lending. And this micro-finance approach must be covenantal. That is, it must operate under the framework of biblical faith and principles and must be fostered through redeemed relationships between the lenders and the entrepreneurs. Initial training and ongoing mentoring must be core components of the lending system, as well as clearly defined lines of expectations and accountability.

Finally, funds repaid can be retained in-country for further micro-lending, under the oversight and management of the Haitians themselves, with the initial U.S. investors and funders acting as business development consultants. This approach provides maximum indigenous control of the resources available, while also creating a relational framework for experienced business people to share their knowledge and wisdom with these budding Haitian entrepreneurs.

*Nebraska-based architect Perry Poyner discusses building site specifics and new orphanage construction concepts with Pastor Jean Paul.*

*Souls Winning staff, orphans, partner pastors, and Reformation Hope staff joyfully watch while Pastor Paul helps set the cornerstone for the new medical clinic.*

*The report of this came to the ears of the church in Jerusalem, and they sent Barnabas to Antioch. When he came and saw the grace of God, he was glad, and he exhorted them all to remain faithful to the Lord with steadfast purpose, for he was a good man, full of the Holy Spirit and of faith. And a great many people were added to the Lord. So Barnabas went to Tarsus to look for Saul, and when he had found him, he brought him to Antioch. For a whole year they met with the church and taught a great many people. And in Antioch the disciples were first called Christians. (Acts 11:22 – 26)*

# CHAPTER X
# Mission Teamwork: Forging Strategic Partnerships

The executive director of Reformation Hope slowly pulled into the parking lot opposite the office building in Marietta, Georgia where his afternoon appointment was waiting. It had already been a very busy week right at the beginning of 2012. One of those kind of weeks in which the meetings, the planning sessions, the travel, and the competing ministry priorities were swirling around his head at a dizzying pace. Just a few days before, he had been in Haiti discussing a new ministry area with Jean Paul — providing some sort of local healthcare for the orphans, the members of the church, and to the surrounding community as well. The sticking point with the whole idea was the same one always encountered by organizations seeking to provide mercy ministries in mission contexts — How in the world was God going to provide the funding?

The Marietta meeting had been arranged several weeks before anything like the idea of a health care ministry had come into view. The meeting was with a regular Reformation Hope partner, the sort of partner who reliably provided a five-figure sum near the end of each fiscal year in support of the mission to Haiti. His foundation, The Invisible Hand, resonated closely with Ref Hope's kingdom vision and areas of ministry.

Once the initial pleasantries were out of the way and these two men began to get down to business, the foundation president looked across his desk at RHI's executive director and said, "I have lately sensed an urging from God to provide for Reformation Hope's ministry in Haiti in a bigger way. Up to now, we have been making these occasional sizable investments in your work. We could just keep on going that way. But I sense that what we would really like to do is a more significant partnership aimed to accomplish a larger project — something with lasting impact in Haiti. And a larger project might just serve to help me teach other donors that it is not a waste of time and money to serve the people in Haiti."

The executive director, now thinking that he should have realized all along the God had arranged the funding he needed before he even knew he needed it, followed up with the obvious question, "Well that certainly sounds interesting to me. Are you sensing the Lord's leading in any sort of specific areas of ministry projects?" Immediately the president replied, "Well the first area that has been on my mind is healthcare. Could we partner with you in creating a hospital or a medical clinic?" And thus Clinique Médicale de le Réforme was born.

Partnering people and organizations is a biblical way to get kingdom work accomplished. Yet both in the United States, which is typically the 'sending' or the 'sponsoring' country, and in Haiti there exists an entirely unbiblical dynamic which encourages working on building individual kingdoms, rather than the kingdom of Jesus Christ. One of the key things that must change in the way that ministry is done in Haiti is the tendency for everyone to guard their own little fiefdom to the detriment of the larger kingdom of God. Christ prayed fervently for a unified and coordinated covenantal family which would prove the truth of the Gospel:

> "I do not ask for these only, but also for those who will believe in me through their word, that they may all be one, just as you, Father, are in me, and I in you, that they also may be in us, so that the world may believe that you have sent me. The glory that you have given me I have given to them, that they may be one even as we are one, I in them and you in me, that they may become perfectly one, so that the world may know that you sent me and loved them even as you loved me. (John 17:20 – 23)

Yet, contrary to the revealed will of the Lord Jesus Christ as presented in the High Priestly Prayer of John 17, believers in Haiti — whether coming from outside the country to serve in missions and relief work, or local Haitians with years of ministry service to their brothers and sisters—excel in working in isolation from one another.

Many Haitian pastors are the masters of their churches and their congregations, entitled to pass along their authority to their sons, their brothers, their nephews, or their cousins as though the body of Christ was a family business. Thus, these men are very protective of their churches, guarding them from permitting other pastors to preach in their pulpits, plant new churches in the community, or partner with others for a larger kingdom goal.

It is also true that the many mission agencies serving in Haiti operate in the same manner as the NGOs and even the Haitian pastors, jealously guarding their compounds, their programs, and the communities over which they wield influence, from the arrival of other new missionaries and sending entities. Although the church of Jesus Christ has been called of God to apply the Gospel to unbiblical patterns in Haiti, it has all too often reinforced this particular sin, ignoring the kingdom unity and cooperation which should serve as an unmistakable mark of the power of Christ's church.

During the period from 2007 to the writing of this work in 2013, there have been at least six evangelical Presbyterian missionaries working in the western areas of Haiti. Each of these missionaries enjoy U.S. support from networks of churches and in most cases from sending organizations like Reformation Hope. Each of them are also operating similar ministry programs: churches, orphanages, schools, pastor training, and healthcare. They also share a vision to develop a system of presbyteries and a national Haitian Presbyterian Church of some sort. And yet, trying to get them all working together—coordinated for a larger kingdom vision for Haiti is nearly impossible. And this represents but a small sample of the many thousands of missionaries and Christian organizations serving in Haiti.

Reformation Hope has made mistakes in this area of kingdom cooperation and must work harder to tear down the walls of suspicion and sometimes jealousy which keep missionaries from joining hands for King Jesus' larger task. Believers serving in Haiti, be they Haitian, American,

Canadian, French, or from some other place, must come to own by God's grace the bigger vision of a Gospel-transformed Haiti.

While RHI has struggled in some cases to engage with other missionaries serving in Haiti, there have also been successes in building kingdom partnerships involving other organizations with shared objectives to achieve project results that would have been impossible without cooperation and teamwork. One of these successes grew out of Reformation Hope's Harvest of Hope agriculture project.

One of the challenges facing Reformation Hope in Haiti was how to assist Souls Winning Ministries in feeding the orphans a healthier diet. Over the course of nine years, the children's food intake had increased from one to two, and more recently, to three meals per day. And yet the bulk of the calories in each meal is derived from the ubiquitous rice and beans, the equivalent of America's bread and potatoes. Ref Hope desired to improve the quality, not just the quantity, of food the children received. It seemed the best solution would be to develop a farm capable of sustaining the dietary needs of the orphanage.

Haiti offers the advantage of three full growing seasons annually, boosting the productivity of a given piece of land over anything the same size in the United States. In the quest for a replenishable food supply through sustainable practices, it was determined that a working farm would yield three key benefits:

1. The sustainably-grown fruits and vegetables planted using one third of the acreage would dramatically improve the variety, the vitamins, and the fiber in the children's diet.

2. An independent revenue stream would be created for the orphanage through growing high-demand cash crops (such as cassava, plantains, and bonitas) using another one third of the farm site.

3. Small business opportunities empowering families from the church community would be created by subdividing the remaining one third of the land into one half and one acre plots made available in exchange for a monthly tithe in produce or currency earned from the plot.

There were two challenges in getting RHI's Harvest of Hope project off the drawing board and into operation. The first challenge was acquiring a large arable land site located within a reasonable distance of the Souls Winning compound in La Plaine. And the second hurdle was maintaining a consistent water supply through an efficient delivery system to enable the farm to take advantage of Haiti's three growing seasons. With the exception of the rainy season from late April to early June, there is not sufficient rainfall across the Haitian western third of Hispaniola to effectively cultivate crops. The all-too-common bucket brigade watering method is ineffective for farms over an acre in size. Thus irrigation has been necessary to profitable Haitian agriculture since the earliest colonial days.

Again God provided answers to both of the challenges. First, he connected Pastor Paul with the mayor of La Plaine and from him Jean learned about a government program to lease land to farmers for an annual fee. The land offered by the Haitian government had once belonged to the Haitian-American Sugar Cane Company (HASCO). It had lain fallow since the day in 1987 that HASCO ceased operations in Haiti with the collapse of the sugar market.[74] The advantages of obtaining cultivation rights to this land included its richness, already existing high-capacity wells, and also the fact that HASCO had engineered a system of irrigation canals and pump stations in order to maximize the water supply available for their sugar cane operations. The mayor took Jean out to the thousands of hectares of abandoned farmland and invited him to select a plot he thought most advantageous.

In the meantime, Reformation Hope obtained two large tractors and other necessary implements and arranged to ship them to Port-au-Prince for Jean's farm team to use on the land. The 70-acre site Jean ultimately chose to lease was about to be cleared and plowed for the first planting

---

74 *The closing of the Haitian American Sugar Company, known as Hasco, put 3,500 mill employees out of work and affected 30,000 to 40,000 small sugar-cane planters in regions around the capital,* Port-au-Prince. The New York Times, April 12, 1987 (posted on-line) http://www.nytimes.com/1987/04/12/world/another-blow-for-haiti-a-sugar-mill-closes.html?pagewanted=1 The company, Haiti's second largest employer, stated *that it was put out of business by sugar smuggled from Miami and from the Dominican Republic.*

of crops when the 2010 earthquake altered the plan. Pastor Paul was told that the Haitian government now intended to build a new international airport to replace the one so damaged by the quake. He and many Haitians already farming plots in that section of the old HASCO fields were told that they had to move to another tract of land. Their farms were about to become Haiti's new airport.

As a result of the land reshuffle, Jean was given another large tract of land further to the east, in an area with an even higher water table and better drainage. And the delay caused by the transition from one site to another was used of God to set in motion his solution to RHI's second challenge ; how to manage the water supply to the crops all year long.

While Pastor Paul was busy dealing with the rebuilding of the Souls Winning compound and negotiating for the replacement farmland site, RHI's executive director was being introduced to the man whom God had prepared to partner with Reformation Hope for irrigating the Harvest of Hope farm, David Youssi, the president of Irrigation Without Borders (IWOB).

Mr. Youssi started this new nonprofit organization with a vision to provide sustainable water supplies to farms and villages in Third World environments. David was impressed by Ref Hope's recent track record in Haiti. He also needed a pilot project for his new organization. Youssi agreed to partner with RHI in order to provide a state-of-the-art S.M.A.R.T. technology irrigation system for the Harvest of Hope project. The cooperative plan called for IWOB to provide the system components and thorough training on installation, operation, and maintenance, while the farm team supplies the labor and takes ownership of the system.

While on a site preparation visit in 2012, Martin Hawley, Jean Paul, and David Youssi arranged a meeting at the U.S. Embassy in Haiti to discuss the proposed agriculture project. They were met at the Embassy by the U.S. economic development officer and by a representative from USAID, a large NGO deeply invested in Haiti, who later connected Ref Hope with the WINNER Project and its director Jean Robert Estimé, son of the former Haitian president, Léon Dumarsais Estimé.

It was agreed with Director Estimé that the Harvest of Hope farm team should receive WINNER's partner organization's Master Farmer training and that Mr. Estimé would take a keen interest in seeing Youssi's pilot project in operation on the old HASCO land. Irrigation Without Borders hopes the pilot project will be successful enough to be replicated with WINNER's approval at many other locations in Haiti.

## Conclusion

As a representative organization of the Lord Jesus and his kingdom, Reformation Hope recognizes the responsibility it bears in partnering with the people of Haiti for Gospel transformation. Part of that responsibility is to apply Gospel principles to areas of the national life which are out of accord with the revealed will of God. RHI also recognizes that there are issues in its own dealings with other mission organizations which must be brought under the light of God's Word.

Clearly the Lord Jesus intends for his redeemed people to work together to get his kingdom built and to bring glory to his name all over the earth. This includes the people of Haiti. When Christian organizations do not work together, but instead work apart and in a competitive manner, Christ is not glorified and the Gospel is not made visible to the receptor culture. Therefore Ref Hope has recommitted itself to seek cooperative partnerships to leverage kingdom resources to build Christ's Church in Haiti.

One of the most recent ways Reformation Hope has challenged its investors and supporters to a higher level of kingdom cooperation is through its involvement in the founding of the North American Haiti Partnership (NAHP). The North American Haiti Partnership is committed to a comprehensive mission, which reads:

*In active collaboration with leaders in Haiti, we are committed to facilitating meaningful involvement of North American local churches and agencies in Spirit-led initiatives that would assist in earthquake relief while at the same time expanding the kingdom of God in Haiti.*

And a simple vision:

*We desire to see the name of Jesus lifted up throughout Haiti.*

With core values promoting biblical kingdom unity:

*The Laussane Covenant statement of faith defines that common bond of NAHP churches.*

*Operate with a spirit of inclusion rather than exclusion.*

*Respect for a variety of perspectives, while seeking the mind of God, will govern our deliberations.*

*Share freely our experience, processes and practices with other like-minded organizations.*[75]

The Christian community can no longer ignore our brothers and sisters, who share the same calling from God to bring the Gospel and its transforming power to the Haitian people. Reformation Hope continues to seek out opportunities to partner with individuals, churches, and other organizations who profess faith in Jesus Christ as the only means of salvation and who desire to offer kingdom message and kingdom mercy ministry to Haitians and also the people of the Dominican Republic.

Recent examples of RHI partnering projects include:

| Project | Partners |
| --- | --- |
| Clinique Médicale de la Réforme (Reformed Medical Clinic) | Samaritan's Purse, NC Invisible Hand Foundation, GA Dixie Salvage, AL |
| New Orphanage Kitchen Facility | The Church of the Messiah, GA |
| Harvest of Hope Farm Project | Irrigation Without Borders, GA |
| Vo-tech School Project | Grace Church, NY Intervision Foods, GA |
| Orphanage Handicapped-equipped Van | Mobility Works, GA |
| Micro-financing Small Businesses | Pacific Crossroads Church, CA |
| New Church and Rebuilt School | Mission to the World, GA |

---

75 Recorded from the North American Haiti Partnership website: http://www.nahaitipartnership.org/who-we-are

*March 2012: Members from the Church of the Messiah and Smyrna Presbyterian Church gather to help load a container bound for Haiti with kitchen equipment, high-powered generator, sports equipment, and musical instruments.*

*October 2013: The Harvest of Hope farm team cut and glue irrigation pipe under the direction of David Youssi, president of Irrigation Without Borders.*

*Even after a massive international relief effort and eighteen months
of heightened NGO involvement, many thousands of Haitians
remained in squalid tent cities.*

*And Jesus came and said to them, "All authority in heaven and on earth has been given to me. Go therefore and make disciples of all nations, baptizing them in the name of the Father and of the Son and of the Holy Spirit, teaching them to observe all that I have commanded you. And behold, I am with you always, to the end of the age."*

*(Matthew 28:18 – 20)*

# CHAPTER XI
## Mission Issues: Short-Term Challenges — Long-Term Solutions

On any given day at Toussaint Louverture International Airport in Haiti packed flights arriving from New York, Atlanta, and Miami flood the immigration area with eager *blanc* Christians excited and anxious to make a difference for Christ. Those interested people-watchers who stand in the newly constructed baggage claim area can simply observe the faces of people coming down the stairway. Wide-eyed and eager, those they watch with curiosity often have no idea about the clash of cultures they are about experience. There is no end to the loudly colored and often creatively designed t-shirts identifying everyone from a particular church or association. There are hoards of fair-skinned, freckled young people, many on their first mission trip outside the States. Sprinkled among them are a few more mature arrivals, perhaps those who have been in Haiti often and have become accustomed to some of the cultural distinctives. Most of them are very *blanc* — that is, very white and very American in appearance, in perspective, and enculturation.

The problem is this. How prepared are these short-term missionaries for the encounters that lie ahead of them? Have they studied the history of the people of Haiti? Have they acquainted themselves with their native tongue, or their customs, or their art and music? Have they considered the longer-term implications or potential impacts of their presence and their engagement with men, women, and children who are part of the

Haitian people group? What happens when their blanc-America meets African-Haiti? What happens when their industrialized and prosperous world collides with Third World desperation, dependence, and poverty?

Clearly there are often cases in which short-term thinking in Haiti missions creates unintended negative impacts — impacts that could have been prevented by applying a long-term kingdom perspective. In the final result, it does not matter how well-intentioned the mission effort may be, if its quantifiable results are largely detrimental to the Haitian people.

So how should servants of Christ be prepared for entering the Haitian mission field? And what long-term perspectives should shape the planning of mission trips, entering missionaries, and partnering organizations? These are the questions that must now be addressed.

## Preparing Missionaries to Enter the Haitian Ministry Field
### Learning Haitian History
Many aspects of preparation for the Haitian mission field resemble those wise training areas used for more than a century in prepping missionaries to enter any field of foreign mission. It is of primary importance, as has been argued in the first chapter of this present work, that the entering missionary has at least a basic grasp of Haitian history, and added to that, its geography and political institutions as well. Perhaps the only thing as complicated and nuanced as Haitian history is its political system — both as it appears on paper *and* how it actually functions on the ground in people's lives.

### Experiencing Haitian Culture
The believer answering God's call to the Haitian people should also seek exposure to Haitian culture, arts, and music. Of course, much of this will happen upon entry into the country and will develop over time. Yet a good introduction to Haitian culture and expected behavior on matters of social intercourse and hospitality will greatly assist the missionary in the early days of labor among the people. For example, in many parts of Haiti is it customary for the appearance of a kiss to be made at both cheeks when greeting a lady. The missionary should be aware of this

because quite often a lady will initiate this greeting, which carries no hidden meaning. Recoiling from the gesture could create a social offense, preventing the missionary opportunities to share the Gospel. There is also the tradition in Haiti of approaching a person's home, knocking on the door, and saying, "Honour." With the owner responding by saying, "Respecte."

## Learning Haitian Creole

Haitian Creole is often declared to be an easy language to learn. Yet some of the Reformation Hope staff have been making the effort to acquire the language with some degree of fluency for some time, without much success. The missionary should at least pick up a Haitian Creole phrase book, perhaps spend time in conversing with an immigrant Haitian Creole speaker from their community, or listen to some Creole audio recordings so as to be able to negotiate at least the greetings and polite questions. As has also been previously noted in this paper in the chapter on preaching in Haiti, ministers and missionaries who believe they are called of God to remain in the country for some time should go deeper in learning, perhaps even mastering the language. One of the volunteers from Pacific Crossroads Church who works with the RHI board, lived on the Souls Winning Orphanage compound for approximately eight months in 2012 and 2013, and in doing so acquired a good working ability in Creole. Immersion with this language is the primary key to approaching fluency. Those who already possess a good command of French will also be able to more effectively negotiate communication in Haiti.

## Preaching the Gospel Narratively

During a recent short-term medical mission trip to the Souls Winning compound undertaken by a team from Harbor Church in San Diego, California, several Haitians professed faith in Jesus Christ after hearing the simple Gospel proclaimed by Harbor's assistant pastor. This was done while the people were waiting in line to see the doctors. Sharing the Gospel is the primary reason believers take up the call and go to a place like Haiti. The Gospel of Christ's kingdom is the foundation for all that Reformation Hope does there as well. God blessed the sharing of the Gospel that week during the medical mission trip. And yet for Sunday worship service proclamation or for Bible studies of other teaching opportunities, it remains essential for the missionary to communicate the Gospel in ways which the Haitian receptor culture can readily grasp. The Gospel preacher in Haiti must be willing to lay aside some of his didactic and argumentative developmental flow and pick up more narrative or story-telling approaches.

## Preparation to Encounter Voodoo and Vodouisants
Work more than a few weeks in Haiti and you will have to deal with the impact of Voodoo on the people of Haiti. It is likely that a resident missionary or pastor will encounter both Vodouisants and Voodoo priests and priestesses (*bokors*, *houngans*, and *mambos*). While these encounters may be unsettling, even frightening to the first-timer, bear in mind that these are people oppressed by the forces of Satan and desperately need to hear the good news of eternal salvation through faith in Jesus. Reformation Hope has seen God convert many Voodoo priests during the seven years working with Jean Paul. And Pastor Paul has also performed exorcisms, driving Voodoo demons out from Haitians in his community. The key is to go prepared and to always be fortified by prayer and by God's Word.

## Cultivating Sensitivity to Common Mistakes Made by Blancs
The entering missionary will also get off to a better start by making himself or herself aware of the cultural mistakes often made by American *blancs* just entering the country. For example, adult men typically do not wear shorts in Haiti in public view. Nor do women wear shorts, short skirts, or revealing tops. It is considered good manners for those teaching classes to Haitians to dress a little more nicely than what would be worn out into the fields or on a trip to the beach. Americans are often approached, especially upon exiting the international airport, and asked for money to help with this or that circumstance the Haitian is facing. It is never a good idea to simply provide a monetary handout when approached. In doing do, the missionary perpetuates the co-dependency

previously described which has so dampened the initiative and creativity of the Haitian people.

Another mistake sometimes made by foreigners entering Haiti for mission or relief work is a tendency to isolate themselves from the very people and the very culture for which they were sent. One report on this, coming from a former foreign aid volunteer who assisted in post-earthquake Port-au-Prince, noted:

> Some organizations, like the U.N. mission to Haiti, restrict their staff's social outings to a pre-approved list of stores, restaurants, and bars subject to vetting by U.N. security personnel. The result is a closely choreographed dance in which most foreign aid workers interact with Haitians exclusively in a few circumscribed patterns: colleague to colleague; patron to server; aid worker to beneficiary. Most foreigners [now] working in Port-au-Prince speak next to no [Creole], have few or no Haitian friends outside of work, and know little of the flavor of local life. In a place where [approximately] 70 percent of the economy is informal, they patronize only businesses in the formal sector, and they experience their social lives in a world that is awkwardly sealed off from the world in which they work.[76]

## Development of Good Emergency, Contingency Planning

Often the last thing people prepare for when leaving to serve in missions — especially those going for a short-term trip comprising but a few days — is an emergency. And Haiti is one of those places where any kind of emergency is unwelcome and often difficult to resolve. It is absolutely essential that anyone traveling to Haiti go prepared. While Reformation Hope has not yet suffered from a serious emergency in-country, one of its partners has dealt with several such episodes in other contexts and has prepared a guide which RHI now recommends to its mission teams. Lee Jacobs and Steve Vereb retell one such example of an unprepared-for emergency which led them to write their guidebook:

> While traveling on an unpaved mountain road in Central America, three members of a mission team were killed when their military

---

76 Amy Wilentz, *Farewell, Fred Voodoo: A Letter from Haiti* (New York, NY: Simon & Schuster, 2013), 188.

style truck rolled over. While this would be devastating enough, it is not the complete story. The first problem was getting help. Thankfully, after some maneuvering, a cell phone had enough signal to reach the U.S. embassy in the capitol, 135 miles and seven driving hours away. A U.S. helicopter initially could not find the team, and after refueling, returned to find the scene of the accident about eight hours after it occurred.

The loss of three lives was overwhelming but that was not the end of this tragic story. The U.S. citizen member of the team who was driving the truck was imprisoned for 30 days until the accident could be investigated. Someone else from the team had to remain in the country to make sure their team member was properly cared for.

Finally, because of lack of comprehensive insurance, the senior pastor told us he spent the next several days working on getting bodies flown back home. Regrettably, he said, these activities kept him from caring for the members of his congregation at home who were desperately in need of their pastor.[77]

Jacobs and Vereb move forward in their preparatory guide from examples of mishaps and tragedies resulting from lack of planning, to defining six foundational principles for a missions crisis prevention program:
1. Missions is a Calling
2. It's not about Safety, it's about Ministry
3. Think Stewardship
4. There is no Prize for being a Risk-Taker
5. There May be a Price to Pay
6. Minimize the Impact of Crisis on the Church[78]

Reformation Hope has adopted the Jacobs-Vereb planning approach in order to reduce the risk exposure to staff and volunteers traveling to Haiti for mission. Team members are required to take out international travel insurance, which includes emergency evacuation and medical

---

77  Lee Jacobs and Steve Vereb, *Going Prepared: A Unique Church-Based Approach to Crisis Prevention for Short-Term Mission Teams* (Maitland, FL: Xulon Press, 2010), 32.
78  Ibid., 37.

treatment. Sending churches are required to have a crisis manager available to coordinate the response in event of an emergency. Those going to the field must familiarize themselves with the country and its dangers. One person on the team is designated as the spokesperson in event of a problem. A first aid kit is necessary as part of the team's gear, as well as a cell phone that will operate on the Haitian network. Water treatment devices such as the Steri-pen are strongly recommended to the team, as water-borne pathogens can be ingested even from bottled water in Third World contexts. And finally a clearly identified team leader is tasked with maintaining basic rules of safety and travel while in the country (i.e. no travel at night and no traveling alone).

## Perspectives that Must Shape Mission Trip Goals and Organization Projects in Haiti
### Gospel Foundation Presented in a "Haitian" Way

Reformation Hope, or for that matter any organization or missionary seeking to bring the Good News of saving faith into the Haitian culture must seek to present King Jesus in ways that are recognizable to Haitians. That is, the perspective must be to learn from Haitian pastors and Haitian Christians the communication styles and methods that will honor their culture, while retaining without compromise the integrity of God's revelation in the Scriptures. This is one of the most challenging perspectives to embrace and to apply for pastors and missionaries coming to Haiti from the United States.

### New *Indigenous* Church Plants

New church planting efforts should be indigenous local movements at inception. Not imposed from outside the country or coerced by *blancs* using financial incentives. The most effective way in which an American sending agency might foster a Haitian church plant is to come alongside after the Holy Spirit has begun the work. And in doing so, the U.S. missional organization should seek out an American church to partner with the new Haitian work. The greatest support the church plant could receive is for covenantal connections to be deeply established between the U.S. pastor and his Haitian counterpart, between the American church's officers and lay leaders and those on the Haitian side, and for the churches whenever possible to visit one another cross-culturally. A good example of a Spirit-birthed and indigenous initiated church plant is the newest RHI work in partnership with Église Presbytérien in La Plaine in response to the people of God in Jacmel, Haiti:

The Église Presbytérien and Reformation Hope sponsored a team in the fall of 2012 to travel from the Souls Winning compound to the southern coastal city of Jacmel. Some local believers in Jacmel had requested that Pastor Paul come to preach the Gospel there and bring along his worship team. Jean rented a tent and a platform and set up an outdoor service over four weeknights in the historic coastal area. By the last night of the services, Jean noticed that even though it was very late, many people were still standing in front of the tent. He learned that they did not want him and his team to leave. Rather they wanted him to stay and start a church in their community. Pastor Paul did not know what to do. The people of Jacmel were joyful for the Word of Christ and many had come to faith during the services. Now some two hundred and fifty of them wanted to start a church. That same night, one of Jean's assistant pastors, Charlot, came to Jean and said, "Pastor, I believe God has called me to plant the new church he is starting here in Jacmel." With that clear sense of God's calling staring him in the face, Jean agreed for Charlot to lead the church planting effort for the city of Jacmel. And the fruit of those first evening outdoor services is a thriving Bible preaching and teaching church of several hundred active members, now seeking a site to build their first church.

## Projects Selected and Planned in Partnership with Local Haitian Leaders and Entrepreneurs

Long-term sustainable transformation in Haiti must ultimately come from within the nation through its God-gifted and God-called leaders and entrepreneurs. Therefore visioning, planning, and implementation of organization programs must begin at the outset to involve local Haitians — even at the highest levels of the process. Why is this so important? Perhaps a lesson learned by one of RHI's partners, HaitiCheri, will serve to demonstrate:

A team of volunteers from HaitiCheri went into the rugged mountains of northern Haiti in order to assist a small village in solving a real problem. The villagers had no nearby source for potable water. Their children and their women (for these are the Haitians who carry water in the culture) carried water by hand, large bucket by large bucket several miles from a source far from the village. The HaitiCheri team thought to themselves, "Oh, we can solve this problem easily for them." They proceeded to dig a deep well and provided it with a pump and some hardware to help the villagers fill their buckets. Before the team of Americans returned home, they had the wonderful joy of watching the women and children walk only a short distance to get their water. And they reflected on how much their project had improved the quality of life for that village.

A year or so later, another team from HaitiCheri was on the ground in northern Haiti and decided to revisit the village to see how things had gone. When they arrived, they could find few women and children and there was no one at the well. They peered into the well and realized it had not been used in sometime. They scratched their heads until a local villager came by and they asked, "What happened to the well?" The villager replied, "Your well broke some time ago. We had hope you would come back and repair it."

HaitiCheri learned the hard way a valuable lesson. That in Haiti, Haitians must be involved in the projects to better their lives or they will not own those projects for themselves. Instead, the grand buildings, the soccer fields, the wells, and the schools will simply be monuments to international charity, still belonging — in the minds of the local Haitians — to the *blancs* who built them.

Reformation Hope takes this lesson very seriously. Thus even the initial investment of capital, as well as labor, prayer, and intellectual property should include and engage Haitians. In most cases, the Haitian contribution will be negligible in terms of actual dollars, but their ability to partner in labor, in prayer, in planning, and in leadership is every bit the equal of anything Reformation Hope may bring.

What kind of outcomes should mission organizations and Christian development groups be seeking for successful projects? Desired outcomes should maximize: Haitian leadership, Haitian ownership, and Haitian vision-casting for new indigenous projects.

A key measurement of success for Haitian partnering projects is the ability for mission or development organizations to disconnect from the project at the appropriate time, leaving a Haitian-sustained work in place. The partnering organization then moving onward to begin the next Haitian partner project opportunity. The fully Haitian-sustained work would then birth other projects as well, yet free from non-Haitian involvement.

## The Challenge of Short-term Haitian Perspectives

There is another challenge involving short-term thinking which anyone entering the Haitian mission field must take into very careful account. Just as foreign missionaries may bring short-term goals and expectations along with them, so also the majority of indigenous Haitian people operate within an extremely short-term framework. This leads to a very unhealthy dynamic in which short-sighted missionaries engage with desperate, just-get-through-the-day thinking Haitians.

The majority of Haitians wake up every morning with one primary thought — one dominating mission — "How am I going to feed myself and my family today?"[79] This most fundamental of daily challenges is on the minds and drives the activities of most of the people rushing along the crowded streets in every city and town. For an out-of-work father or a mother preoccupied with putting together a few *gourdes*[80] to buy a simple, single meal for their family, long term, even mid-range thinking, visioning, and planning is virtually impossible.

In order to minister to the Haitian facing this dominant challenge, missionaries and agencies must understand this deeply imbedded and instinctual fixation upon daily survival. This dynamic will reside in the background of every cross-cultural interaction and conversation that takes place with a poor Haitian.

---

79  Haitians often speak of the daily search for work/food as "making life."
80  The Haitian *gourde* is a unit of currency which is measured against the U.S. dollar. Typically the *gourde* is valued between 30 and 40 to 1 U.S. dollar.

And it will explain why a Haitian may not show up for an agreed-upon meeting, or for a class, or even for some type of special event. Feeding himself and his family will overrule everything else. This is a huge and often dividing difference of perspective between Haitians and Americans.

It is because of this that while the missionary is sharing the Gospel and working toward longer-range project outcomes, he may yet be required to provide some short-term relief in terms of food and water. The goal is to remove the immediate crisis from the Haitian's life in order to allow him to begin to focus on the Gospel of Jesus, and on preparing and planning for tomorrow's needs today.

*Once completed, the medical clinic will be managed by and employ several Haitian staff, and minister to the pressing needs of the local community.*

*Pacific Crossroads Church has provided funding and negotiated training for the new block-making business venture, which is vital to the success and cost-savings of our medical clinic construction project.*

*Pastor Paul explains the process of formalizing a new church to the Jacmel leadership team, shown here underneath the simple tent used for their worship services. Pastor Charlot, the church planter, can be seen standing to the left.*

*This is why I left you in Crete, so that you might put what remained into order, and appoint elders in every town as I directed you— if anyone is above reproach, the husband of one wife, and his children are believers and not open to the charge of debauchery or insubordination. For an overseer, as God's steward, must be above reproach. He must not be arrogant or quick-tempered or a drunkard or violent or greedy for gain, but hospitable, a lover of good, self-controlled, upright, holy, and disciplined. He must hold firm to the trustworthy word as taught, so that he may be able to give instruction in sound doctrine and also to rebuke those who contradict it.*
(Titus 1:5 – 9)

# CHAPTER XII
## Mission Transformed: An Indigenous Way Ahead

What will Reformation Hope's mission in Haiti look like in three to five more years? What lessons learned may be applied for the benefit of others planning to enter the Haitian culture to proclaim the Gospel? How should Ref Hope proceed in partnering with brothers and sisters, and with churches and organizations such that Christ is glorified and the kingdom of heaven advanced? These are the questions addressed in this concluding chapter.

### Lesson 1: Indigenous-led and indigenous-owned is essential.
For Reformation Hope this means the expansion of the microfinance initiative. It also means that increased decision-making by Haitian leaders is a desired outcome in all Reformation Hope's ministry and development project areas. And the indigenous-led commitment requires that all church planting arise from indigenous local interest, not imposed from outside the region or outside the country.

### Lesson 2: Indigenous trainers are the goal of leadership and pastor training.
RHI's leadership development must be conducted in-country, as opposed

to traditional outside-of-country models. For Reformation Hope this means the development of degree granting theological programs, the rise of degreed Haitians teaching the courses, and the reduction of *blanc* authority while empowering local leaders.

## Lesson 3: Disaster relief must yield as quickly as possible to non-dependent approaches to development.

For Reformation Hope this means equipping Haitians to address hurricane or earthquake events with more local resources, internal leadership, and response structures. The lesson of the January 2010 earthquake disaster is that while outside emergency relief is effective for immediate distress, longer-term rebuilding must be driven by the Haitians themselves. There is no doubt, based upon Haiti's geography and position in the Caribbean, not to mention past history, that it will suffer from periods of severe hurricanes (as in 2008). Seismologists are also convinced that Haiti may be entering a more active tectonic period. Prudence dictates that RHI develop a disaster plan for the future in conjunction with Souls Winning Ministries, and that Souls Winning be strengthened and prepared to respond in-country.

## Lesson 4: Local sustainability must be in view as the criteria for success of all economic partnering.

For Reformation Hope this means strengthening vocational-technical training through the new Souls Winning vo-tech. This presents a special challenge in terms of procuring qualified and reliable instructors for the technical training classes. It also means broadening sustainable agriculture initiatives such as the Harvest of Hope, and instilling motifs of economic independence through the micro-finance business model. As the Zafen organization focuses upon lending to established businesses, Reformation Hope and Souls Winning Ministries must seek out another micro-finance partner for those Haitians who are pioneering start-ups.

## Lesson 5: Mission ministry must be carried out within the framework of covenantal relationships.

In the early days of RHI's partnership with Souls Winning Ministries in Haiti, more of the planning and management of projects was carried out by the Americans. God blessed the efforts despite the imbalance in executive leadership roles. If placed upon Corbett and Fikkert's "Participatory Continuum," Haitian involvement with RHI in projects was somewhere between the "Compliance" and the "Consultation" modes.[81] Now Reformation Hope sees the essential and biblical value of full collaboration between the Haitian leadership of Souls Winning and the decision-makers in the U.S. with Ref Hope. And yet the best outcome will result when Reformation becomes a consistent "Responder" to Haitian "Community Initiated" agendas.

A new era defined by an "equalization of roles" is now underway. Reformation Hope prefers for the indigenous Haitian partners to identify ministry opportunities and to initiate project concepts and goals. The biblical rationale for this leveling of roles and even subordination of U.S. authority to Haitian direction is the recognition of mutual redemptive authority in the kingdom of Christ.

For Reformation Hope this means developing the next generation of Haitian leaders is absolutely essential — of the very highest priority — just below that of proclaiming the Gospel. So that these young leaders in turn will become involved agents of change and driving visionaries for the direction of ministry and the creation of programs within their country. With the Gospel of the kingdom as their foundation, they will be used of God to transform every field of calling in their country — from ministry to government to science to the arts — all redeemed by the blood of the Lamb. Along the way to this lofty vision, Reformation Hope must delegate more and more of the management — more and more of the final authority and ownership of its projects to Haitians, including goals, design, utilization, staffing, record-keeping, and assessments of success. Reformation Hope sees itself as a base of support for God's instrument in Haiti, Jean Jacob Paul, who has been called of God, as was Timothy, *to put what remains into order, and appoint elders in every town.*

---

81  Steve Corbett and Brian Fikkert. *When Helping Hurts: How to Alleviate Poverty without Hurting the Poor... and Yourself* (Chicago, IL: Moody Publishers, 2012. Originally published 2009), 140.

*November 2013: The hired workmen at the Haiti Customs facility unload the Reformation Hope container and transfer the contents into the holding container. The supplies remained sealed in the customs yard until the load was valued and the import fees were paid by Souls Winning.*

*I rejoiced in the Lord greatly that now at length you have revived your concern for me. You were indeed concerned for me, but you had no opportunity. Not that I am speaking of being in need, for I have learned in whatever situation I am to be content. I know how to be brought low, and I know how to abound. In any and every circumstance, I have learned the secret of facing plenty and hunger, abundance and need. I can do all things through him who strengthens me.*
*(Philippians 4:10 – 13)*

# CHAPTER XIII
# Epilogue: Mission Customs and Mission Crises
# October — November 2013

## Mission Customs

Nothing Reformation Hope had previously learned in dealing with the Haitian customs process prepared their executive director for what he encountered when he arrived with Jean Paul and some of his team at the shipping container facility in Port-au-Prince. After a brief wait in line, the men were issued guest I.D. badges and permitted into the secure cargo container processing area. Inside the secure area, they waited for some time in order for the customs official assigned to the container to appear. When she appeared, they were directed to a loading dock area specifically designed for processing shipments into Haiti for customs evaluation. The customs officer took her seat next to the doors of Ref Hope's shipping container, which was the last in a long row of similar containers — some already being unloaded and assessed. Jean was required to hire a team of eight Haitian laborers necessary to unload the container. These men work under the supervision of Haitian customs and are paid on the spot in cash when each container is unloaded.

While Americans might be tempted to think that their container would be unloaded and assessed, then released to its owner, that is not how it works. In this case, the Haitian customs office requires the container be unloaded — each item checked and recorded for future customs valuation — then reloaded into an adjacent container. The new container is resealed and then stored again at the cargo facility until the customs fees have been assessed and paid. The fees assessed include the price of delivering the container to the customer's property when the process is completed.

It was good thing that Jean, Ref Hope's executive director, and several of Jean's assistants, arrived for the container inspection. Since they were on-site and were also taking pictures, no one attempted to help themselves to items they might have wanted. However, the group of men watched as from the containers immediately adjacent to theirs, unloading workers removed tires (highly prized apparently) and also opened a barrel filled with t-shirts and passed them out among the other laborers and a customs inspector! Over the course of the hours it took to unload their container, the team observed a tidy pile of slightly used tires accumulating beside them. Later on, some of the workmen bartered and traded for the tires that they wanted to take home with them. Needless to say, when the Souls Winning hired workers emerged from the Reformation Hope container carrying brand-new $300-apiece Goodyear Kevlar tires, everyone along the entire dock took notice. By God's grace, nothing went missing from the Ref Hope shipment to Souls Winning, and only one item was seriously damaged — a sink intended for one of the clinic bathrooms.

Dealing with the customs process in Haiti is always complicated and it is usually expensive. It is very important when shipping items into Haiti via container that shippers have a relationship with an expediter in Port-au-Prince. As the above true story indicates, it is also essential that either the organization shipping the container, or the recipient, be present for the valuation of the cargo and its transfer from the shipping container to the customs holding container. Not to do so would be to invite the distribution of some of the most valuable items into the hands of those tasked with unloading, instead of the hands of those for whom it was intended.

# Mission Crisis 1

On October 5, 2013 Jean Paul emailed the executive director of Reformation Hope with some bad news. It had started raining heavily on Friday the fourth, so the farm team was not at the Harvest of Hope acreage. During the day, with the land unattended, a large group of local villagers and some Haitian police arrived with sledge hammers, machetes, ropes, and some trucks and proceeded to pull down both the Souls Winning fencing and Director Estimé's WINNER[82] fencing. They also tore down about half of the large building that Estimé had nearly completed. Jean was very, very upset.

The next Monday, Pastor Jean drove Reformation Hope's executive director from the airport to the farmland in order to show him the damage to Souls Winning's agriculture project and the destruction inflicted upon Director Estimé's building and fences. The two arrived around 1:30 p.m. While there, they were met by one of Estimé's agronomy supervisors, who was directing WINNER's farm laborers. After some conversation back and forth about what had happened on the previous Friday and who was behind it, he warned them to get out of the area as soon as possible. He told Jean, "There is going to be a lot of trouble here around 3 o'clock."

Sensing that the warning was indeed serious and that land conflicts in Haiti often get violent, they hopped into Jean's SUV and drove away from the farmland. On the way out, they stopped at a little family-run drink stand to get water and Cokes. While sitting there in the vehicle, another SUV drove up the road and stopped beside them. Three brawny Haitian men inside gave them the once over and glared at the two as though they were in their sights for certain trouble. All the while the owner of the drink stand was softly but firmly urging Jean to take his passenger and leave at once. Soon, however, Jean and his passenger watched them as the threesome finally began to drive away — heading right out to the land where the two had been standing and talking not long before.

---

82 The month before, Haiti WINNER had signed a lease with HASCO to cultivate the lands adjoining the Souls Winning property in the fertile farming area outside of Marin/LaPlaine. Thus Director Estimé's organization began developing all of the available plots surround those farmed by Jean Paul's farm team.

About 5:00 p.m that day, while driving in Marin, Jean turned on the radio and was amazed. He turned to his American partner and said, "Martin, it is very unusual for newspeople in Haiti to cover violence that occurs out on the land late in the day. That is why the villagers want to stir up trouble after 3 p.m. The news media typically won't cover a late story—it gets dark too soon, it's muddy, and it's more dangerous. But this news reporter is saying that after we left the land today there was heavy fighting between the villagers who live near our farm and some people who support WINNER. It was very serious. Six people are dead and fourteen have been wounded!"

Apparently the clash developed out on the land because the local villagers and small farmers were frustrated that much of the open range-land had been leased by Haiti WINNER and by Souls Winning. As a result, the locals, who had been accustomed to freely accessed, open land for grazing their animals, felt threatened with so many acres now converted to farming and fenced-off from the public.

Thank God that he delivered the Souls Winning farm team from harm's way on the previous Friday. And the Lord was certainly at work again on the next Monday, as he delivered Jean Reformation Hope's executive director from being caught in a crossfire, while the two opposing sides fought it out over the rights to use the farmland.

Reformation Hope's Harvest of Hope ministry now finds itself caught in the middle of a land rights dispute, a very common problem in the nation of Haiti. It is a dispute over whether or not HASCO, the Haitian American Sugar Cane Company, still has the right to lease the land it once used for cultivating sugar cane. On the one side the local villagers say "no", and maintain their right to manage acreage they see as communal in nature, while on the other side the local mayor and the WINNER organization say "yes." Which side will win? Only time and God's purposes will tell, because thankfully the conflict has moved from hot lead on the open range into the Haitian court system. In Haiti, the litigation process for such a hotly-contested dispute could take years to reach a final resolution.

In the meantime, this episode has convinced the board of directors of Reformation Hope that it is time to begin raising support for the purchase of farmland for the Harvest of Hope project. As with other development projects in Haiti, Ref Hope would act as the grantor of funds to Souls Winning Ministries, who in turn would be the legal Haitian owner of record for the land. With Jean Paul's organization possessing clear title to arable land in the La Plaine area, the Harvest of Hope agriculture project, with all of its bright promise for the future, would be able to move forward, most likely without serious interruption. This would be a tremendous benefit to the children of Jean's orphanage, as well as to the expansion of Irrigation Without Border's mission to help the people of Haiti with S.M.A.R.T. water technology.

## Mission Crisis 2

About 1:00 p.m. on Friday, November 8, 2013, without prior notice or warning, four large trucks, two or three pickups, and some smaller vehicles pulled up to the Souls Winning compound in La Plaine and some sixty heavily armed Haitian National Police entered the compound escorting an official magistrate. The judge came armed with an Eviction Judgment and his men began removing church property from the sanctuary. He ordered everyone — men, women, and the orphans — out of the compound. While the children of the orphanage were shaking with fear and some were crying loudly, Pastor Jean interrupted his pastor training seminar and came out to confront the judge. What in the world had brought about this crisis? As with virtually everything that happens in Haiti in the here and now, its roots lay in a turbulent past:

On February 7, 1986, Jean-Claude Duvalier (Baby Doc) departed Haiti, via a U.S. Air Force aircraft, for exile in France. With his departure amidst great civil unrest, many other Haitians, who had served his government or who were considered his friends, felt that in order to save their lives and families they too must flee the country. Among those who left in February of 1986 were a father and mother and three children. Like Duvalier, they fled to France and began new lives in their place of exile.

While this family was away from the country, a powerful man named Mr. Osias took over their lands (plots totaling twenty-seven acres) and held unto them for some twenty years. While hard to understand for

Americans accustomed to the United States and its safeguards concerning land ownership, this is a frequent occurrence in Haiti. In the meantime, the father and mother of the exiled family living in France passed away. Throughout these decades, the family deemed it unsafe to return to Haiti, let alone to reassert their title to the disputed lands.

Near the end of this twenty year period, Mr. Osias met Pastor Jean Paul and in 2007 virtually gave much of the land for the current compound to Souls Winning Ministries. He also sold the adjacent house to the ministry for forty-five thousand dollars. Mr. Osias' attorney provided proper legal paperwork for transferring the claim on the land from him to Jean Paul's ministry. A title form was provided, but title verification was not conducted by going to the Haitian land recording office to check the original file. Souls Winning Ministries received much of the current compound land as a gift from Mr. Osias, and in good faith assumed he was the legitimate title holder.

Eventually, Mr. Osias received Christ but then succumbed to prostate cancer. He died away from his homeland while seeking medical treatment in France. However, he left instructions in his estate specifying his offer to sell the house and the remaining land which went with it to Souls Winning Ministries for forty-five thousand dollars plus closing costs. Pastor Paul, with help from his Reformation Hope partners, was able to purchase the land at this bargain price — the house being worth well over one hundred fifty thousand dollars.

Souls Winning Ministries thus acquired during 2007 all of the land for the current compound for the token sum of eleven thousand dollars, as well as the two-storey house, for the equivalent of forty-five thousand dollars plus the closing costs. Over the ensuing seven years, Souls Winning Ministries with Reformation Hope's assistance and others, has expended some five hundred thousand dollars in building a wall, a deep well, a reservoir, a commercial kitchen, a school, a church, an office, a storage building, and bathrooms on the site.

Fast forward to 2013. Jean-Claude Duvalier returns to Haiti and with little interference resumes his life as though much of the past had never happened. As a result, other families who had fled into exile felt that they too could safely return. The surviving children from that family who fled in February 1985 — two brothers and a sister, now grown-up — return to Haiti and reassert their claim to the title for all of the acreage previously occupied by Mr. Osias. Part of that acreage is the location of the Souls Winning Ministries main compound.

The returned siblings filed their claim with the special Haitian court division tasked with handling title disputes. For some unknown reason which is now under investigation, Jean Paul is never notified to appear in court while the magistrate is assessing the case. As it turns out, the two brothers and their sister can demonstrate their family's ownership of the land going back to 1908. And further, although many of the original paper land title documents were destroyed when the 2010 earthquake leveled the government building, the title deeds to these specific plots of land survived intact. The originals exist and are available for inspection by the court. The family received a favorable judgment against all of those currently using the disputed lands, not just the acres used by Souls Winning. In their efforts the expatriate family was aided by the current Haitian Minister of Justice, who is a close friend of the children's relatives.

After the magistrate described the eviction judgment and the nature of the original owners' complaint, Jean immediately contacted his attorney, who thankfully was nearby. Jean's attorney, Mr. Joseph Manes Louis, is a former Attorney General of Haiti under both Jean-Bertrand Aristide and also René Préval. Mr. Louis arrived on the scene quickly and immediately began negotiating with both the judge and also the attorney representing the two brothers and sister. Thanks to his efforts, the children, the staff, and the brothers and sisters of the congregation were not evicted from the property on that terrible day.

The result of the negotiations as it stands at present are these:

1.  The price originally demanded for Souls Winning Ministries to purchase the land was lowered from $650,000 to $250,000.
2.  Rather than immediate payment or eviction, Jean's attorney managed to get a ninety-day timeframe before final action is taken — February 7, 2014.
3.  Mr. Louis is working on a further extension of the time allowed before the sale must be complete.

Jean has also challenged his congregation in strong terms to partici-
pate in the redemption of this land by sacrificially giving toward its proper
purchase. This is similar to the approach used when the compound was
rebuilt after the 2010 earthquake. Many of the local church members gave
modest offerings and also lent their labor to the project, thus becoming
heavily invested personally in its success.

This severe crisis, which threatens the stability of the orphanage and
the large church congregation that meets at the compound, has reminded
the Reformation Hope and Souls Winning organizations that they are
engaged in both spiritual and physical warfare against the forces of evil
so entrenched in Haiti. While the family threatening Souls Winning's
presence on the current compound may indeed by legally entitled to
compensation for their land, their actions through the Haitian legal
system have greatly disrupted ministry momentum and the development of future mission projects in the country.

Reformation Hope and Souls Winning Ministries know by faith, and
by years of experience, that God will indeed provide for his children
according to his lavish mercy. As of the completion of the first edition of
this book, it is yet to be seen precisely how God will supply this $250,000
need. But the Lord has never left his orphaned children and has repeat-
edly provided for this mission exceedingly, abundantly beyond all that
anyone could ask or even imagine. Perhaps the Lord will also mightily
use this book as an instrument to overcome this crisis, as all royalties
earned with the sale of each book will be given in support of Reformation
Hope's "Save the Orphanage" fund.

Perhaps this crisis could have been avoided, or at least mitigated,
had Souls Winning and Reformation Hope been more experienced and
mindful of the inherent instability of land ownership is Haiti. This trial
has certainly taught the staff of Reformation Hope just how fragile and
tenuous land titles can be in Haiti. *At any given time somewhere in
Haiti, there are land disputes stemming from conflicting claims of
ownership. It would not be an exaggeration to suggest that the historical inability of the Haitian state to develop low-cost enforcement of
real-estate property rights is the second most important source of*

*Haitian underdevelopment.*[83] Careful land office research, as well as obtaining title insurance, is essential for any further support of Souls Winning Ministries in acquiring land. This is a cautionary tale for anyone seeking to establish ministries in Haiti, such as churches, orphanages, guest houses, or medical clinics which involve the purchase of land.

In the first place, there have been eras in Haitian history when the nation's constitution forbade foreign ownership of land. For example, *back in 1867, a Haitian writer had called it the "Holy Grail" of the country's liberty, and the provision was still tremendously popular half a century later.*[84] The prohibition does not exist at the present time but could be reinstated with very little advance notice. Yet even the current provisions allowing foreigners to own Haitian land come with limitations. As one real estate website reports:

> The Haitian system of establishing property rights is so convoluted, complicated and corrupt that for the average citizen of Haiti, owning any property will always remain just a dream. Obtaining a legally recognized title to property in Haiti takes over 11 years and 111 bureaucratic steps involving 32 separate offices and countless forms to be filed, according to Hernando de Soto's "The Mystery of Capital".

> Foreigners may not own more than one residence in the same district or own real estate without authorization from the Ministry of Justice. Land holdings of foreigners are limited to 1.29 hectares in urban areas and 6.45 hectares in rural areas. Additionally, foreigners may not own property or buildings near the border.[85]

It is therefore important that organizations in need of land for projects seek to partner with a Haitian organization in whose name the land will be titled. Other groups have worked within the Haitian system by

---

83  Jean-Germain Gros, *State Failure, Underdevelopment, and Foreign Intervention in Haiti* (New York, NY: Routledge, 2012), 80.
84  Laurent Dubois, *Haiti: The Aftershocks of History* (New York, NY: Metropolitan Books, 2012), 244. Despite the fact that every Haitian constitution adopted since independence in 1804 forbade non-Haitian land holding, in 1918, under the auspices of U.S. military and political pressure, a new constitution permitted foreign ownership of land.
85  http://www.globalpropertyguide.com/Caribbean/Haiti

obtaining government donated plots where important community benefits will occur — such as with medical clinics or hospitals. These options are preferable to seeking to acquire land solely as a foreign entity in Haiti.

Secondly, organizations purchasing land, or partnering with a Haitian-managed entity to buy land, should perform all due diligence with respect to verifying the seller's valid title and unencumbered ownership. It has been reported that perhaps as little as 5% of the land in Haiti has clear, undisputed title records.

Finally, land transactions in Haiti are handled a cash sales. There are no mortgage companies or banks offering real estate loans. Prices are often comparable to those found in major U.S. cities. American buyers cannot expect to find cheap, Third World bargains in Haitian real estate. In fact, Haitian sellers typically expect to receive a premium from what they perceive to be wealthy American buyers. It is therefore essential for many reasons to hire a Haitian attorney to represent your organization in the negotiations, the sale, and for the transfer of title.

*Jean Paul reviews the damage to the farm fencing, as well as the building destruction suffered by the Haiti WINNER organization.*

# The Beauty of Haiti

# Bibliography

Anglade, Boaz. "The Forgotten Earthquake Victims: Neglect Outside of Metropolitan Port-au-Prince." In *Journal of Haitian Studies*, Claudine Michel, ed., vol. 16, no. 2, Fall 2010, pages 4 – 18. Santa Barbara, CA: Haitian Studies Association and the Center for Black Studies Research, University of California.

Braun, Bob. "Haiti Orphanage Pastor with N.J. Ties Endures with Hope Amid Earthquake Destruction." In *Star-Ledger* on-line edition, January 15, 2010, 1:10 pm. http://blog.nj.com/njv_bob_braun/2010/01/haiti_orphanage_pastor_with_nj.html

_____ "Late Supper Spares 56 Children at Haiti Orphanage from Church Collapse." In *Star-Ledger* on-line edition, January 15, 2010, 10:00 pm. http://blog.nj.com/njv_bob_braun/2010/01/dinner_delay_spares_56_childre.html

Belgarde-Smith, Patrick. "Uprisings, Insurrections, and Political Movements: Contemporary Haiti and the Teachings of History, 1957 – 2010." In *Haiti Rising: Haitian History, Culture and the Earthquake of 2010*, Martin Munro, ed., 134 – 144. Kingston, Jamaica: University of the West Indies Press, 2010.

Clitandre, Nadège T. "Haiti Exceptionalism in the Caribbean and the Project of Rebuilding Haiti." In *Journal of Haitian Studies*, Claudine Michel, ed., vol. 17, no. 2, Fall 2011, pages 146 – 153. Santa Barbara, CA: Haitian Studies Association and the Center for Black Studies Research, University of California.

Corbett, Steve and Brian Fikkert. *When Helping Hurts: How to Alleviate Poverty without Hurting the Poor ... and Yourself*. Chicago, IL: Moody Publishers, 2012. Originally published 2009.

Curnutte, Mark. *A Promise in Haiti: A Reporter's Notes on Families and Daily Lives*. Nashville, TN: Vanderbilt University Press, 2011.

Dayan, Joan. *Haiti, History, and the Gods*. Berkeley, CA: University of California Press, 1995.

Desmangles, Leslie G. *The Faces of the Gods: Vodou and Roman Catholicism in Haiti*. Chapel Hill, NC: University of North Carolina Press, 1992.

DeTellis, Timothy. *Haiti: Past, Present, and Future — Where Is the Hope?* Altamonte Springs, FL: Advantage Books, 2010.

Dubois, Laurent. *Haiti: The Aftershocks of History*. New York: New York: Metropolitan Books, 2012.

Dumas, Reginald. "Haiti at the Intersection of the World: Tapping the Past, Facing the Future." In *Journal of Haitian Studies*, Claudine Michel, ed., vol. 17, no. 2, Fall 2011, pages 124 – 145. Santa Barbara, CA: Haitian Studies Association and the Center for Black Studies Research, University of California.

Engel, James F. and William A. Dyrness. *Changing the Mind of Missions: Where Have We Gone Wrong?* Downer's Grove, IL: InterVarsity Press, 2000.

Farmer, Paul. *Haiti After the Earthquake*. New York, NY: PublicAffairs, 2011.

_____ . *The Uses of Haiti*. Monroe, ME: Common Courage Press, third edition, 2006. Originally published, 1994.

Felix, Emmanuel. *Understanding Haitian Voodoo*. Maitland, FL: Xulon Press, 2009.

Fievre, M. J. "No Funeral for Nono." In *So Spoke the Earth, Ainsi parla la terre Tè a pale: a Haiti anthology*, edited by M. J. Fievre, 73 – 77. South Florida: Women Writers of Haitian Descent, August 2012.

Frechette, Richard. *Haiti: The God of Tough Places, the Lord of Burnt Men*. New Brunswick, NJ: Transaction Publishers, 2012.

Garrigus, John D. "The Legacies of Pre-revolutionary Saint-Domingue." In *Haiti Rising: Haitian History, Culture and the Earthquake of 2010*, Martin Munro, ed., 115 – 125. Kingston, Jamaica: University of the West Indies Press, 2010.

Gauthier, Amélie and Madalena Moita. "External Shocks to Fragile States: Building Resilience in Haiti." In *Fixing Haiti: MINUSTAH and Beyond*, Jorge Heine and Andrew S. Thompson, eds., 27 – 40. Tokyo, Japan: United Nations University Press, 2011.

Geggus, David Patrick. "Saint-Domingue on the Eve of the Haitian Revolution." In *Haitian History: New Perspectives*, Alyssa Goldstein Sepinwall, ed., 72 – 88. New York, NY: Routledge Press, 2013.

_____. *Haitian Revolutionary Studies*. Bloomington, IL: Indiana University Press, 2002.

Greer, Peter and Phil Smith. *The Poor Will Be Glad: Joining the Revolution to Lift the World Out of Poverty*. Grand Rapids, MI: Zondervan, 2009.

Gros, Jean-Germain. *State Failure, Underdevelopment, and Foreign Intervention in Haiti*. New York, NY: Routledge, 2012.

Hayes, Donna-Marie. *Touching Haiti...A Medical Mission Story*. Boise, ID: Saint Alphonsus Foundation, 2001.

Henningfield, Diane Andrews, ed. *Perspectives on Modern World History*. Farmington Hills, MI: Greenhaven Press, 2013.

Herlinger, Chris and Paul Jeffrey. *Rubble Nation: Haiti's Pain, Haiti's Promise*. New York, NY: Seabury Books, 2011.

Jacobs, Lee and Steve Vereb. *Going Prepared: A Unique Church-Based Approach to Crisis Prevention for Short-Term Mission Teams*. Maitland, FL: Xulon Press, 2010.

Jacobs, Lee. Haiti— "Forgotten Already?" In *The Permanente Journal*, Fall 2010, vol. 14, no. 3, 80 – 81.

Jennings, J. Nelson. *God the Real Superpower: Rethinking Our Role in Missions*. Phillipsburg, NJ: P & R Publishing, 2007.

Katz, Jonathan M. *The Big Truck That Went By: How the World Came to Save Haiti and Left Behind a Disaster*. New York, NY: Palgrave Macmillan, 2013.

Laferrière, Dany. *The World Is Moving Around Me*. David Homel, trans. Vancouver, CA: Arsenal Pulp Press, 2011.

Louis, Bertin M., Jr. "Haitian Protestant Views of Vodou and the Importance of *Karactè* Within a Transnational Social Field." In *Journal of Haitian Studies*, Claudine Michel, ed., vol. 17, no. 1, Spring 2011, pages 211 – 227. Santa Barbara, CA: Haitian Studies Association and the Center for Black Studies Research, University of California.

Lundahl, Mats. *Poverty in Haiti: Essays on Underdevelopment and Post Disaster Prospects*. New York, NY: Palgrave MacMillan, 2012.

Lupton, Robert D. *Toxic Charity: How Churches and Charities Hurt Those They Help (And How to Reverse It)*. New York, NY: HarperCollins Publishers, 2011.

Magloire-Sicarde, Suzy. "Earthquake." In *So Spoke the Earth: a Haiti Anthology,* edited by M. J. Fievre, 149 – 153. South Florida: Women Writers of Haitian Descent, Inc., 2012.

Métraux, Alfred. *Voodoo In Haiti*. New York, NY: Schocken Books, 1972. Reprint of original, published 1959.

Myers, Bryant L. *Walking with the Poor: Principles and Practices of Transformational Development*. Maryknoll, NY: Orbis Books, 2011. Revised from original edition of 1999.

Nakhla, David P. "Short-Term Missions: Pros and Cons." In New Horizons, edited by Danny E. Olinger, vol. 34, no. 4, April 2013, 19 – 22. Willow Grove, PA: The Orthodox Presbyterian Church.

Nicholls, David, "Rural Protest and Peasant Revolt, 1804 – 1869." In *Haitian History: New Perspectives*, Alyssa Goldstein Sepinwall, ed., 180 – 196. New York, NY: Routledge Press, 2013.

Nicholson, Charles H., M.D. "Chronology of Onset of the Haitian Cholera Epidemic: October and November 2010." In *Journal of Haitian Studies*, Claudine Michel, ed., vol. 16, no. 2, Fall 2010, pages 38 – 47. Santa Barbara, CA: Haitian Studies Association and the Center for Black Studies Research, University of California.

Pascual, Christine, M.D. *Out of My Comfort Zone: A Journey Into the Medical Mission Field of Haiti*. Bloomington, IN: CrossBooks, 2012.

Podur, Justin. *Haiti's New Dictatorship: The Coup, the Earthquake, and the UN Occupation*. London, UK: Pluto Press, 2012.

Satterthwaite, Margaret L. and P. Scott Moses. "Unintended Consequences: The Technology of Indicators in Post-Earthquake Haiti." In *Journal of Haitian Studies, Special Issue on Education and Humanitarian Aid*, Fabienne Doucet and Jody A. Dublin, guest editors, vol. 18, no. 1, Spring 2012, pages 14 – 49. Santa Barbara, CA: Haitian Studies Association and the Center for Black Studies Research, University of California.

Schuller, Mark. *Killing with Kindness: Haiti, International Aid, and NGOs*. New Brunswick, NJ: Rutgers University Press, 2012.

_____ and Pablo Morales, *Tectonic Shifts: Haiti Since the Earthquake*. Sterling, VA: Kumarian Press, 2012.

Schwartz, Timothy. *Travesty in Haiti: A True Account of Christian Missions, Orphanages, Food Aid, Fraud, and Drug Trafficking*. San Bernardino, CA: Privately Published, 2nd edition, 2010. Originally published 2008.

Sepinwall, Alyssa Goldstein. "From the Occupation to the Earthquake: Haiti in the Twentieth and Twenty-First Centuries." In *Haitian History: New Perspectives*, Alyssa Goldstein Sepinwall, ed., 215 – 240. New York, NY: Routledge Press, 2013.

Shenk, Wilbert R. *Changing Frontiers of Mission*. Maryknoll, NY: Orbis Books, 1999.

Trouillot, Evelyne. "Eternity Lasted Less Than Sixty Seconds..." In *Haitian History: New Perspectives*, Alyssa Goldstein Sepinwall, ed., 312 – 316. New York, NY: Routledge, 2013.

Trouillot, Michel-Rolph. "An Unthinkable History: The Haitian Revolution as a Non-Event." In *Haitian History: New Perspectives*, Alyssa Goldstein Sepinwall, ed., 312 – 316. New York, NY: Routledge, 2013.

Wainwright, Babette. "Do Something for Your Soul, Go to Haiti." In *The Butterfly's Way: Voices from the Haitian Dyaspora in the United States*, edited by Edwidge Danticat, 204 – 208. New York, NY: Soho Press, Inc. 2001.

Wilentz, Amy. *Farewell, Fred Voodoo: A Letter from Haiti*. New York, NY: Simon & Schuster, 2013.

Wright, Dave. "Mwen se Ayiti." In *Vwa: Poems for Haiti*, edited by Lisa Marie Basile, 33 – 34. Caper Literary Journal Charity Project, CreateSpace Independent Publishing Platform, March 16, 2010.